PRELUDE TO FRANCO

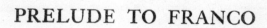

By the Same Author:

VENEZUELAN PROSE FICTION, New York, 1933

DILLWYN F. RATCLIFF

University of Cincinnati

PRELUDE TO FRANCO

Political Aspects of the Dictatorship of General Miguel Primo de Rivera

•

Preface by Saul K. Padover

•

LAS AMERICAS PUBLISHING COMPANY

New York

ACKNOWLEDGMENT

The author wishes to express his gratitude to all who have aided him in the preparation of this book. For both advice and encouragement he is particularly indebted:

to members of the Graduate Faculty of Political and Social Science of the New School, New York City;

to colleagues at the University of Cincinnati;

to Anne Harrington Ratcliff;

and, especially, to Dr. Saul K. Padover of The New School, whose unfailing interest and kindness have also led him to write the Preface to this book.

It goes without saying that none of these people is in any way responsible for errors of fact or interpretation which may be found herein.

The map of the military regions of Spain was prepared by Elizabeth Dalvé.

Printed in the United States of America
by Las Americas Press, Inc.

To the Memory of

Dr. Boris Mirkine-Guetzévitch,

Scholar, Teacher and Friend

PREFACE

Dr. Ratcliff's book—part biography, part history—is an interesting study of that usual Iberian phenomenon, the "unpolitical" politician. Primo de Rivera, who seized power about a dozen years before Franco, was in the Spanish tradition of the uniformed man-on-horseback. He shared with numerous predecessors, as well as some successors, those characteristics which have long made Spain the most backward and most poverty-stricken country in Western Europe. Primo was ignorant, inflexible, rigidly militaristic, proud, and, of course, authoritarian. He was as much use to a Spain that had been struggling to emerge into the twentieth century as, say, the efflorescence that in the Middle Ages went by the name of the "king's evil."

Not that Primo was either evil or cruel. On a personal level, indeed, he was a decent person, as dictators go; and as dictators go, he went. He went along the deep-trodden path of petrified authoritarianism.

In one sense, Dr. Ratcliff's fascinating study of Primo, that inept and hopelessly benighted dictator, is an exercise in the old adage of *plus ça change plus c'est la même chose*. For Primo was a true product of the Spanish landed aristocracy, with its grim roots in a past that, elsewhere in Western Europe, has gone out with the Age of Reformation. Primo, the nobleman, the General, the dictator, had his intellectual being in another world. He operated on the categorical assumption that 1923, the year of his military coup, was no different from 1493, when Ferdinand and Isabella had set up *their* brand of autocracy.

To some extent, Primo was, of course, right. Spain had not changed much since the day when the Aragon-Castile dynasty burnt heretics and books and, through the Inquisition and the *Index Librorum Prohibitorum,* destroyed all freedom. But it had changed some. Spain, its intellectual life wrecked at the end of the Middle Ages, had slumbered through the rest of Europe's great ages of scientific enlightenment. Nevertheless, there were signs of awakening in our times. Many Spaniards, among them intellectuals and labor leaders, began the heartbreaking process of waking up a decayed and illiterate nation. There were some experiments with Parliamentary government, with some institutions of freedom, even with republicanism. All these hopeful efforts finally came to nothing.

Why? A long time ago, Jefferson, with his usual acuteness, put his finger on Spain's fundamental trouble. "Spaniards," he said, "are too heavily oppressed by ignorance and superstition for self-government." It was men like Primo de Rivera and his successor, Franco, who took advantage of the benightedness of their people to destroy all attempts to educate them and bring them a measure of freedom. Dr. Ratcliff's scholarly and lively book on Primo is an invaluable contribution to an understanding of the ways and whys of Spanish dictatorship.

SAUL K. PADOVER
New School for Social Research
New York, February 3, 1957.

CONTENTS

PUBLISHED WITH THE AID OF

THE CHARLES PHELPS TAFT MEMORIAL FUND

UNIVERSITY OF CINCINNATI

INTRODUCTION

TWICE during the first half of the twentieth century the Spanish Army achieved the conquest and occupation of Spain. In September, 1923, General Miguel Primo de Rivera's bloodless putsch was at once successful. In July, 1936, Spanish Army officers revolted under the leadership of General Francisco Franco and, although aided both by the active intervention of the fascist powers and by the indecisiveness of the democracies, were able to overthrow the Spanish Republic only after nearly three years of bitter civil war.

Political developments under the two unconstitutional and dictatorial régimes show a number of striking similarities. The two generals were confronted with almost identical problems and difficulties. Upon attaining power, Primo de Rivera sought to fill the political void by creating an apolitical monopoly of patriotism, known as the Unión Patriótica. Under General Franco's Spanish State, political monopoly has been bestowed upon the one recognized party, the Falange Española Tradicionalista. In each case, a movement headed by a general stopped the political clock in Spain. But each régime's monolithic organization soon began to lose prestige due to factional strife, corruption, and favoritism.

Each dictator has endeavored to establish by fiat the legality and presumptive constitutionality of his rule. Primo, after five years of extra-legality, undertook to supersede the suspended Constitution of 1876 with the Draft Constitution of 1929. Similarly, a half-dozen of Franco's decrees have been declared "Fundamental Laws of the Spanish State." In his quest for evidence of popular support, each general has also had recourse to nation-wide plebiscites and referenda.

To substantiate further its claimed right to rule, each régime has tried to establish moral justification for the revolt which brought it to power. Primo maintained that he was saving Spain from anarchy and politicians,

1

in the name of law and order and the monarchy. Franco's Cruzada undertook to "defend Christian civilization against red barbarism." Primo fell from power when growing dissatisfaction within the Army caused royal approval to be withdrawn. General Franco has been more astute; only a few murmurs of dissent have, so far, been heard within the Army. As regards the monarchy, Franco has preferred to be a regent ruling on behalf of a vacant throne. This has enabled him to play against one another the different monarchist factions, and all of them against anti-monarchist elements within the Falange. In order to strengthen its rule, each government set up rigid control of foreign trade, of the press, and of the universities.

Dictators like to think they are indispensable, and therefore immortal. Primo often spoke of retiring from power "in a few years," but made no serious effort to provide for succession to his post. He resigned only when it was made very clear to him that he had lost control of the Army. Generalissimo Franco, in a decree of July 26, 1947, first solemnly declares himself Chief of State, then adds that he may name his own successor, or, if he does not, a monarch or another regent shall be chosen by the Regency Council, the Council of the Realm, and the Cabinet ministers. In other words, Franco also has thus far failed to answer the question, "Who's next?"

However, to expect political events in Spain today to repeat the pattern of thirty years ago would be naive. The story of Primo de Rivera's dictatorship is to be viewed rather as bringing into focus basic conditions and fundamental problems which are essential factors of life and politics in General Franco's Spanish State today.

PART ONE

BACKGROUND OF EVENTS
AND ATTITUDES

SPAIN: CHRONOLOGY 1788-1939

Bourbon Dynasty in Spain, 1700-1931

1788-1808 Reign of Carlos IV.

1789-1794 French Revolution.

1807-1808 Occupation of Spain by Napoleon's troops.

1808 May 2. First uprising in Madrid against the French.

1808-1813 Spain's War of Independence. "The Peninsula War" against the French, by the Spanish people and the British army under Wellington.

1808 Joseph Bonaparte, King of Spain.

1808-1826 Successful Wars of Independence of the Spanish colonies in America.

1810-1813 The liberal Cortes of Cádiz and the Constitution of 1812.

1814-1833 Fernando VII, King of Spain.

1823-1833 Spain an absolute monarchy under Fernando VII.

1830 The birth of Fernando's daughter (María) Isabel; confusion concerning Carlos IV's abrogation of the Salic Law provides the pretext for the Carlist movement and Wars of 1834-39, and 1872-76.

1833 Death of Fernando VII, end of absolutism; return to Spain of exiled liberals.

1833-1840 Regency of María Cristina, widow of Fernando VII, in the name of Isabel II.

1834-1839 First Carlist War: the Pretender Don Carlos (brother of Fernando VII) against Isabel II (daughter of Fernando VII).

1841-1843 Regency of General Baldomero Espartero, in the name of Isabel II.

1843-1868 Isabel II on the throne.

5

1868-1870 Provisional government of General Francisco Serrano Domínguez.

1870-1873 D. Amadeo of Saboya was King of Spain.

1872-1876 Second Carlist War.

1873-1874 First Spanish Republic. Presidents: Estanislao Figueras, Francisco Pi y Margall, Nicolás Salmerón, Emilio Castelar.

1874 Spanish Restoration of the Bourbon dynasty.

1874-1885 Reign of Alfonso XII, son of Isabel II.

1876-1931 Constitution of 1876.

1885-1902 The "Pact of El Pardo," providing for alternation in power of Práxedes Sagasta's "Liberals" and Antonio Cánovas' "Conservatives."

1885-1902 Regency in the name of Alfonso XIII, of his mother, María Cristina, Archduchess of Austria.

1892 Anarchist farm laborers attack Jerez de la Frontera in Andalusia.

1892 Barcelona bombing and assassinations by anarchists are encouraged or condoned by Catalán nationalists seeking to weaken and discredit the central government; also by employers, by the central government, by the police, and by reactionaries seeking excuse for martial law.

1898-1899 War with the United States. Loss by Spain of Cuba, Puerto Rico, and the Philippines.

1902-1931 Reign of Alfonso XIII.

1906 March. Law of Jurisdictions requires courts martial for all Spaniards accused of offences against the Army or the Fatherland.

1909 July. During the "Tragic Week," Semana Trágica, in Barcelona, opposition to military service in the Moroccan War causes a general strike, riots, martial law, and executions.

1913 Law of Mancomunidades permits regional self-government.

1914-1918 World War I. Spain is neutral and Spaniards are divided in their sympathies.

1917 General strike in Madrid and Barcelona. Anarchist strikes in South and East.

1919-1923 War of the Barcelona gun-men.

1921 At Annual, Spanish Morocco, General Fernández-Silvestre's forces are annihilated by Abd-El-Krim's Riffian Moors.

6

1923-1930 Dictatorship of General Primo de Rivera.
1925 Abd-El-Krim defeated; Morocco pacified by joint action of the Spanish troops, under General Primo de Rivera, and of the French forces.
1930-1931 "Dictablanda" of General Dámaso Berenguer.
1931-1939 Second Spanish Republic.
1933-1935 "Black Biennium" of reaction.
1934 October. Uprisings in Catalonia and Asturias.
1936 February. People's Front wins election.
1936-1939 Spanish Civil War.
1940-1945 World War II. Falangist Spain is "non-belligerently" pro-Axis.
1939- The Spanish State of General Francisco Franco, the Army, and the Falange Party.

I. Military Career of Miguel Primo de Rivera

M IGUEL Primo de Rivera y Orbaneja was born on January 8, 1870, and died on March 16, 1930. His birthplace was Jerez de la Frontera, the city of sherry wine, in southern Spain. Throughout his life it was always evident that Don Miguel was an Andalusian and that he belonged to an "Army family."

Jerez was also the home-town of his mother, Doña Inés Orbaneja y Pérez de Grandellana. His father's name was also Miguel, Don Miguel Primo de Rivera y Sobremonte, and he was from Seville. He had been a lieutenant colonel of cavalry and a staff officer, but before the birth of little Miguel, the sixth of his eleven children, he had retired from the army, and was devoting himself to the management of his rural estate near Jerez. Hence, on his son's baptismal certificate, he modestly terms himself *labrador,* farmer.

Fernando, one of the brothers of Don Miguel junior, was also an army officer and died in Morocco in 1921, a most disastrous year in Spanish military history.

The person who most influenced the young Primo de Rivera, as hero, pattern, preceptor, and sponsor, was his uncle, Don Fernando Primo de Rivera y Sobremonte, 1831-1921. Uncle Fernando was a lieutenant general, captain general, and field marshal, who had served in the second Carlist War of 1868-76 and in Cuba, as well as in the Philippines, where he had been governor general. A member of the Cortes and a Senator, he had also been Minister of War in 1907 and again in 1917. Distinguished service in the Carlist War had brought him the title of Marqués de Estella, a title which his nephew inherited after the old general's death in 1921.

Don Miguel's social background was, then, that of Andalusian landed gentry and his life pattern that of the Spanish Army officer.

At the age of ten, young Miguel was sent to Madrid to live at the home of another uncle, Don José, who was also an army officer. For four years he attended various academies in the capital, which prepared him for admission to the Academia General Militar in Toledo. He received his commission as second lieutenant upon his graduation from the Academy in 1888.

A first lieutenant since the age of twenty, he was, in 1893, serving in the Melilla area of Spanish Morocco with the 15th Infantry Regiment, also called the Extremadura Regiment. (Spanish regiments, and even battalions, often have names as well as numbers.) Courageous recovery of a piece of artillery which seemed to be about to fall into the hands of the Moors won for Lieutenant Primo de Rivera the coveted military Cross of San Fernando. [1]

In 1895-96 Don Miguel served in Cuba and was promoted to major. He went to the Philippines in 1897, as aide-de-camp to his uncle, Don Fernando, who was then returning to the islands, after an absence of fourteen years, in the combined capacities of captain general and governor general.

After some service in the field, Don Miguel, now a lieutenant colonel, represented his uncle, the Governor General, in negotiations with the Filipino revolutionary leader, Emilio Aguinaldo. The final terms of surrender were considered too generous by many Spaniards. Aguinaldo and 34 members of his staff were transported to Hong Kong, released, and

10

given 400,000 pesetas. Less than a year later, in May 1898, Aguinaldo returned to the Philippines at the invitation of the Americans, who had just destroyed the Spanish fleet in Manila Bay.

In 1902 Don Miguel married Casilda Sáenz de Heredia, by whom he had six children. She died in 1908 and he did not remarry. His son, José Antonio, was the founder and, until his execution in 1936, the leader of the Falange Española. Another son, Miguel, and his daugther, Pilar, have been active in the Falange party and in the affairs of Generalísimo Franco's Spanish State.

Don Miguel was stationed in the Peninsula from 1898 to 1909. In 1908, when he was thirty-eight years old, he was promoted to colonel. In 1909 he participated in the war against the Moors in the Melilla area of eastern Spanish Morocco. In 1911 he was wounded in action along the Kert River, was decorated and sent back to Spain, and promoted to brigadier general. In 1913, now a major general, he returned to Africa, but this time to the Tetuán area in western Morocco.

During the years of World War I, Don Miguel was military governor of the important Cádiz area but he was transferred after two years because of outspoken criticism of the then government and its conduct of the Moroccan campaign. He went with a Spanish military mission to view the French and British front in 1917. In 1919 he became a lieutenant general. In that same year he showed some moral courage when, in Zaragoza, he opposed certain policies of a sort of military officers' union called a *Junta de Defensa.*

In 1920 he was captain general of the Third (Valencia) Military Region and, briefly, of the First (Madrid) Military Region. He lost this latter position because at this time in his career he was an outspoken *abandonista,* that is, he believed that Spain should withdraw from Morocco completely. As a

11

corollary to this view, he held that Spain should offer to trade the North African city of Ceuta to England in exchange for Gibraltar. But these views were not popular in government circles.

In 1922 Don Miguel was Captain General of the Fourth (Barcelona-Catalonia) Military Region and it was this position that he held when he carried out his military coup of September 1923.

12

II. Personality of the Dictator

WHAT manner of man was this lieutenant general who felt that he had been called to save Spain? Miguel Primo de Rivera began life with the quadruple disadvantage of noble birth into a landowning Andalusian Army family. It is true that, to some slight extent at least, he did rise above the usual Spanish connotations of the words *noble, landowning, Andalusian,* and *Army.* Gerald Brenan, the British gentleman farmer, who lived in southern Spain for many years, says of the General:

> Primo's own personality was not an unattractive one. He was an Andalusian landowner from Jerez: the province where a hard-drinking, whoring, horse-loving aristocracy rules over the most starved and downtrodden race of agricultural labourers in Europe. It is a region where the hatred of the poor for the rich has been accumulating for generations. But Primo evidently did not share the feelings of his set. All his actions show a desire to remedy the condition of the poor, within the rather narrow framework of what was possible to him.[2]

Don Miguel always loved wine, women, gambling and politics, as well as song. Of him the Madrileños were wont to say:

> "Naipes, mujeres y botella
> son el blasón
> del Marqués de Estella."

13

"Cards, women and a bottle are the heraldry of the Marquis of Estella." Indeed, a most characteristic trait of his was the fatuous optimism of the incorrigible gambler. One of the Tharaud brothers quotes the General as saying, in the spring of 1925: "Difficult problems? Nothing is difficult. There is no difficulty." Then the French publicist adds:

Et ce mot m'éclaira d'une vive lumière l'homme que j'avais devant moi. Son optimisme n'était pas un optimisme de commande. C'est l'optimisme du joueur qui a de l'estomac et qui sait aussi qu'il a la chance. (3)

Primo de Rivera's two outstanding qualities were his sincere patriotism and his astounding conceit. Patriotism saved him from the worst forms of that social particularism so prevalent among both Army officers and members of the landowning nobility, a situation which has been well characterized by José Ortega y Gasset in his *Invertebrate Spain*. (4)

The dictator's vision of Spain was comprehensive enough to include, along with the nobility and the Army, the unaffiliated common people, and especially the members of the socialist sponsored trade unions of the *Unión General de Trabajadores* (UGT). On the other hand, he never entirely overcame the prejudices of his class toward anarcho-syndicalists among the Andalusian rural proletariat, and toward the middle class merchants, intellectuals, and politicians. His slogan was *Patria, Religión, Monarquía,* but the first was ever paramount. Catholicism and the dynasty were merely convenient stabilizing factors in society.

General Primo de Rivera's vast conceit made him proud of most of his defects. The man actually boasted of his ignorance, of his "ability to improvise," of his lack of dignity and self-discipline. Conceit made him opinionated, overly self-confident, impatient with dissent and disagreement. Conceit kept him convinced of his popularity with the Spanish people

14

and with his fellow Army officers long after that popularity had ceased to exist. Don Miguel was also very proud of his prose style and of his oratorical ability. The intellectuals made fun of the dictator's florid harangues and verbose statements to the press. As a would-be intellectual himself, Don Miguel forgot his pose of magnanimity and began a furious campaign of harassment against writers, journalists, professors, and university students. However, belief in his own grandeur, even when in error, made it possible for him to admit his mistakes and to change his mind completely. This is a trait almost unheard-of in dictators and generals. Before coming to power, Don Miguel was an *abandonista* as far as Spanish Morocco was concerned. He also favored Catalonian regional autonomy until he came to power and realized that it threatened Spanish unity. On each of these issues he did a sudden about-face.

The rise and fall of Don Miguel as dictator shows that the greater handicap is to be "Army" in Spain. Primo de Rivera had picked up many enlightened ideas, but he was still influenced by the Spanish Army world with its instinctive praetorianism. The Spanish military mind is rigid, hierarchic, demands decision, does not tolerate reflection, discussion, or criticism, and regards the civilian as a sub-human menace. Primo de Rivera's favorite civilian organizations were the *Somatenes,* militia companies of Catalonian origin. His Military Directory, September 15, 1923, to December 3, 1925, contained eight brigadier generals, representative of the eight military regions of Spain. During the same period, most of the mayors and provincial governors appointed by Primo were Army officers. When the dictator finally fell from power it was because the highest-ranking officers answered evasively his circular letter asking whether they approved his régime.

Impatient with any opinion except his own, Primo served as universal Minister of the Realm during the Military Directory, using as secretaries and assistants the eight generals and the one admiral associated with him. His obsession with "unity"

15

caused him to be partial to the theoretically monolithic Army, in which a purely literal and material parade-ground uniformity delights the heart of the military martinet. That the monolithic social group is an illusion was something that Infantry General Primo de Rivera was to learn the hard way, through his difficulties with the Artillery officers. He also undertook to have all patriotic civilians organized into one apolitical "movement," *la Unión Patriótica.*

In addition to his Army-mindedness, Primo had a second capital defect: he held the by-no-means-uncommon belief that politics is evil and that all politicians are wicked conspirators against the Fatherland and its patriotic citizens. He wrote:

> Politics. Is politics necessary to the life of peoples? Is politics a mere discipline or speculative academic study, aiding in the training of him who is to govern, like Economics and Law, or is it an essential factor indispensable in the governing of peoples? I believe it is the former, and therefore, that the Parliament, the Government's highest organization of collaboration, investigation, and evaluation should not be of a political nature, but should be made up of eminent personages, representing the different sectors of national life, who, without previous affiliation, organization of parties, or recognition of leaders, act on each occasion in accordance with their judgment and conscience, granting or refusing their approval to the limited number of bills which the governments should submit to Parliament, and offering to those governments the fruit of their studies and undertakings, with complete independence of governmental action. This is my conviction and that of the Patriotic Union, and this I propose to bring to the spirit of the laws which the Government over which I preside will soon submit for the consideration and approval of His Majesty and to the vote of the people.[5]

This prejudice against parliamentary politics and politicians was, of course, reinforced by the attitudes of the landed gentry and the Army officer caste toward the upstart bourgeoisie: traders, money lenders, anticlericals, republicans and other sinners.

16

It is not surprising, but it was unfortunate, that Primo de Rivera, a clever man of good will, should have been the victim of two such tremendous fallacies: (1) his inability to conceive of society except in terms and patterns of military organization, and (2) a fanatical distrust of politics and an implacable hatred of politicians. But for these two defects, Don Miguel, who had actually been a Senator, might have had a useful career as an able, affable, and rather enlightened politician.

Indeed, aside from his Army and his anti-political preoccupations, Don Miguel had a remarkably open and supple mind. So much so, that the Spanish Falangists of today, with condescending tolerance, forgive him for being contaminated by nineteenth century liberalism! (6)

III. Land, Labor, Capital—and the Military

Dᴜʀɪɴɢ the century preceding World War I, the landholding oligarchy was, economically and politically, the most powerful social group in Spain. This class was almost continuously the power behind the government, whether the current Premier was one of Antonio Canovás' "Conservatives" or one of Práxedes Sagasta's "Liberals". Although these two pseudo-parties systematically alternated in power and plunder, they served the same master. Many of these landholding families were of the aristocracy, others belonged to the upper middle class. But they all sought from the political parties, the Army, and the monarchy protection for their law, order, property, and prestige. [7]

Other important elements of Spanish society were:

1) the merchant class, whose members often favored free trade, and were frequently anticlerical republicans or constitutional monarchists;

2) the industrial and finance capitalists of Catalonia, who demanded high protective tariffs and who had created Catalonian separatism as a weapon to be used against the central government in Madrid, and also as a demogogic means of preserving their control of the middle class in Catalonia. These powerful interests supported Primo's coup, and felt that they had been betrayed when the dictator later opposed Catalonian separatism

3) the anarchists and anarcho-syndicalists who dominated the labor movement of the Barcelona area and who also provided ideology and leadership for much of the rural proletariat of landless Andalusian peasants; [8]

4) The Socialist Party and the socialistic General Labor Union (UGT, *Unión General de Trabajadores*). These organizations were comparatively strong in central Spain and among the workingmen of the cities, except in Catalonia and Andalusia. Primo de Rivera respected and favored the Socialists because of their organized discipline and because their interests clashed not with those of his class, the landowning gentry, but with the interests of the urban bourgeoisie. In the main, the Socialist Party adhered to the position of its leader, Indalecio Prieto, and did not collaborate with the dictatorship. However, the General Labor Union, under the leadership of "Don" Francisco Largo-Caballero, was represented on four different governmental bodies set up by the dictatorship. [9]

The Spanish Army was, and still is, primarily a political entity, but it was divided. First, there was King Alfonso's military household, a political machine with the King as boss. There were also differences of opinion and interest between the company and field officers on the one hand, and the generals on the other. In June of 1917, the infantry officers organized *Juntas Militares de Defensa,* a sort of Army officers' Soviet. Many of these infantry officers were of middle class family. They complained that, in terms of promotions and rewards, they did not receive their due, and that the palace generals caused the King to grant disproportionate favors to the more aristocratic artillery and engineer corps officers. Although Primo de Rivera opposed the *Juntas,* the fact that he was an infantry general later increased his difficulties with the artillery officers.

20

Subsequent to the Spanish Army's defeat at Annual on July 21, 1921, by Abd-El-Krim's Berber tribesmen, General Juan Picasso's report fixed immediate responsibility for the disaster upon thirty-three Army officers. These revelations, as well as further information that might be uncovered by an investigating commission of the Cortes, would almost certainly disclose King Alfonso's personal responsibility for the disaster. For, impatient of constitutional restraint, and convinced of his own genius as a strategist, the monarch had ignored both Premier Manuel Allendesalazar and the Viscount of Eza, Minister of War, by encouraging a stupidly reckless and headstrong royal favorite, General Manuel Fernández-Silvestre, to attack the Moors without waiting for orders from his superior, General Dámaso Berenguer, High Commissioner of Spanish Morocco. Both Monarch and Army were angered and terrified by the rising clamor for the fixing of "responsibilities." To prevent damaging revelations, they had recourse to the military coup of September 13, 1923, in Barcelona.

IV. The Barcelona Manifesto of September 1923

THE Manifesto of the *coup d'état* was dated at Barcelona, September 12, 1923, and was signed by Miguel Primo de Rivera as Captain General of the Fourth Military Region. It was addressed "to the country and to the Army." The General expressed regret at having been compelled to depart from legality at the behest of patriotic Spaniards who held that their country's salvation demanded that it be freed from the professional politicians responsible for a quarter century of national disgrace and misfortune.

The military would fix responsibilities and, in the meantime, they would either govern Spain themselves or else place power in the hands of civilians "who represent our morality and doctrine."

After brief, lyrical hurrahs for Spain and the King and for the virility of the rebellion, the General presented, as justification for the coup, a list of political ills and social evils, viz.:

1) the murder of prelates, ex-governors, civil oficials, employers, foremen, and workmen,

2) bold and unpunished hold-ups,

3) depreciation of currency,

4) the squandering of millions of pesetas from special funds,

5) a dubious and dishonest customs policy,

6) political connivings to exploit the Moroccan tragedy,

7) indecisiveness in confronting that very serious national problem,

8) social indiscipline which makes labor inefficacious and which destroys industrial and agricultural production,

9) impunity of communist propaganda,

10) impiety and misbehavior,

11) political interference in the administration of justice,

12) shameless propaganda pro regional separatism,

13) subversive passions with regard to the problem of responsibilities.

After this impressive list of sins of omission and commission, the General's sense of humor caused him to credit the last constitutional government, that of Manuel García-Prieto, with one little good deed during the nine months of its existence: a feeble attempt to suppress gambling! Then he continued:

> We have not come to bewail shame and disgrace, but to apply a prompt and radical remedy, for which we demand the support of all good citizens. To this end, and by virtue of the confidence and mandate given me, there will be constituted in Madrid a military Directorate of Supervision and Inspection, *un Directorio inspector militar,* of a temporary character, charged with maintaining public order and insuring the normal working of the Ministries and official bodies, exacting of the country that, in a short time, it offer us men upright, wise, industrious, and honorable, who can constitute a Ministry under our auspices, but with complete independence of action, in order that we may offer them to the King if he sees fit to accept them.
>
> We do not wish to be ministers nor have we any ambition other than that of serving Spain. We are the *Somatén,* the organized militia of legendary and honorable Spanish tradition, and, like it, we have as our motto, Peace, peace, and peace! But that means an honorable peace abroad and, at home, a peace based upon salutary severity and just punishment. Let there be neither betrayal of principle nor impunity.[10]

24

His reference to the *Somatén* was metaphorical, but mental association caused the General to take himself literally and it occurred to him that a national militia could be a political as well as a military "reserve," so he called for the organization of the *Gran Somatén Español.*

Primo de Rivera could not see how any man of good will could possibly want to oppose his movement but, if there should be opposition, it would be ruthlessly crushed.

In the following paragraph he declared, "We are not imperialists," and added that, in Morocco, the Army had vindicated its honor, and hinted at the possibility of a peaceful settlement there: "We shall seek for the Moroccan problem a solution that will be prompt, worthy, and reasonable!"

He then brushed aside the demand for the fixing of responsibilities for the military disaster in Morocco and added that, instead, the military would hold the politicians and the parties responsible for injuring and disgracing the fatherland. To this end, he invited evidence from informers. He added specifically that Santiago Alba, Minister of Foreign Affairs in the García-Prieto government, would be brought to trial, as would also Manuel García-Prieto himself, for his responsibility as Premier for the acts of his subordinate, Don Santiago.

The dictator then stated that law and order would be maintained throughout Spain under the direction of the captains general of the eight Military Regions, who would depose the civil governors of all provinces. The duties and authority of these civilian officials would be taken over by the Military Governors and commanding officers. The military would seize all means of communication, all public utilities, banks, railway stations, prisons, etc., as well as all centers of potential subversion and resistance.

The final paragraphs attempted to justify the seizure of power. The General and his associates had not conspired, they were giving organized implementation to the will of all patriotic Spaniards. He remarked that he did not consult the lower ranks of the military lest discipline be impaired. The General then added:

> Although we may come into being through an act of technical indiscipline, we do represent that true discipline which is due our principles and love of country, and so we shall conceive, practice, and require discipline, not forgetting that, since we are moved not by ambition but, on the contrary, by the spirit of sacrifice, ours is the highest authority. [11]

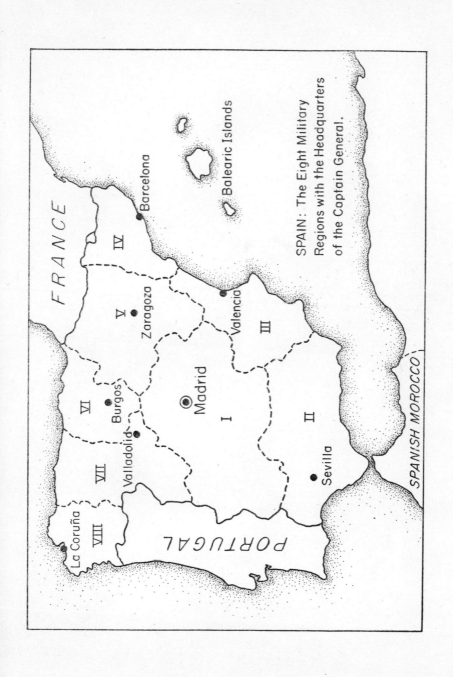

FRANCE

Barcelona

Balearic Islands

IV

V
Zaragoza

Valencia

III

VI
Burgos

Madrid

I

II

Valladolid

VII

Sevilla

VIII
La Coruña

PORTUGAL

SPANISH MOROCCO

SPAIN: The Eight Military
Regions with the Headquarters
of the Captain General.

V. Military Directory and Ministerial Dictatorship

THE government of Manuel García-Prieto resigned without protest on September 14, 1923, and, on the following day the dictator announced that he would be assisted by eight brigadier generals, each representing one of the eight military regions into which peninsular Spain is divided, and one admiral, representative of the Navy. An Army colonel served as secretary of this Military Directory.

The Constitution of 1876 was suspended and the Cortes suppressed as unnecessary and useless. Two months later, lest there be an attempt to convene a new Cortes, the permanent stand-by commissions of both houses were suppressed.

All ministries of the national government were suppressed; their salaries were eliminated from the budget, because the brigadier generals, who had replaced them, were on the army payroll; ex-premiers and ex-ministers lost their pensions and were also forbidden to serve as directors or counsel of corporations.

A series of decrees followed. The elective local township governments (*ayuntamientos*) were dissolved and their places taken by army officer delegates of the military dictatorship; similar military appointees took over the county circuits (*partidos judiciales*). As a further means of destroying the power of local bosses, military inspectors visited 815 township governments and preferred charges which led to the dismissal of 152 township secretaries and 121 clerks. [12]

A decree of January 13, 1924, dissolved all provincial legislatures except those of Navarra and the Basque provinces in northern Spain. Thus, in a period of four months, the structure of the state was altered and most of its instrumentalities, except the Army and the Civil Guard, were dismantled.

When Primo de Rivera staged his coup in Barcelona, he had the enthusiastic support of most Catalonian separatists and autonomists. Within three months, however, he had realized that Catalonian separatism was divisive and subversive of national unity, and was not to be tolerated.

Most Spaniards, whether friendly or opposed to Primo de Rivera, gave the dictator credit for bringing the Moroccan war to a successful conclusion. This was presumably a matter within the General's field of competency. First, during the year 1924, he shortened the line, although it meant giving up no fewer than 180 hard won outposts, including the Moors' holy city of Xauen. In addition to what strategic ability he may have had, he was lucky: the Levante wind did not blow on the morning of September 8, 1925, and the Alhucemas amphibious operation, near what is now the town of Villa Sanjurjo, was successful. His greatest piece of good fortune came when an overconfident Abd-El-Krim attacked both Spanish and French Morocco, thus cutting off the arms which the French had been glad to see sold to him as long as they were used to kill only Spaniards! With the help of the French, and after much hard fighting, the Riffian tribesmen were defeated and, on May 27, 1926, Abd-El-Krim chose to surrender to the French, who sent him to the island of Reunion.

In the meantime, domestic political developments of some importance had taken place. As a result of growing dissatisfaction in Spain, the dictator had dismissed the eight generals and the admiral who constituted his Military Directory and, on December 3, 1925, had installed a Ministerial Dictatorship of civilians. But Primo de Rivera was, in fact, the one and only universal minister and, as commanding general, he permitted the nine "ministers" to play the roles of staff members, aides-de-camp, or mere orderlies.

General Primo considered his movement entirely apolitical and sought the support of the Monarchy and the working class. He soon realized that the King was an uncertain ally, whose waning prestige might make him a political liability. The labor leaders, in so far as they collaborated with him, never lost sight of their own objectives. It is natural, then, that his temperament and inclination, as well as a superficial view of the realities of the situation, should cause him to rely chiefly upon the Army, the Navy, the national constabulary (*Guardia Civil*) and the customs guards (*Carabineros*). Of these armed "institutes," the Army was the decisive factor. But even the Army was divided and restive. The officers of the Artillery and Engineer Corps, as well as the naval officers, considered themselves the social superiors of the Infantry officers—and Primo was an infantry general. Even so, he was on bad terms with other generals, Dámaso Berenguer, for instance. Many field and company officers in the infantry disliked him because of his opposition to their *Juntas de Defensa* (Officers' Associations). In addition, the front line officers in Morocco, especially those of the Spanish Foreign Legion, had special interests and grievances. Indeed, as early as July 19, 1924, the dictator, still inclined to pull out of Morocco, was confronted with a near riot, almost a mutiny, when he spoke of falling back to a new line of defense.

The conspiracy of November 1925 was easily suppressed, but it is significant that it was led by two generals and two colonels. More serious was the *Sanjuanada,* the Saint John's Day coup, of June 1926, a more comprehensive undertaking in which were involved aristocrats, capitalists, generals, and anarchists. The Socialists refused to cooperate when the leaders refused to agree to overthrow the monarchy as well as the dictatorship. "That would be going too far," said Count

Romanones in answer to Francisco Largo-Caballero's blunt question. As a matter of fact, the representatives of the landed and monied oligarchy wished to sacrifice the dictator in order to save themselves by preserving the monarchy. [13]

The conspirators lacked decisiveness and energy and there was no bloodshed. Primo punished them by imposing upon them extra-legal fines in proportion to their means. [14]

But even more serious were the difficulties which Primo was having at this time with the artillery officers. In that corps it was a tradition of long standing that a cadet, on being commissioned, took a solemn oath that he would only accept promotion by seniority. In order to gain control of this corps, Primo tried to force the artillery officers to accept the usual system of arbitrary, special, or "merit" promotions.

The artillerymen protested, refused, were suspended by Primo, and finally had recourse to mass resignations. On the last day of 1926, these officers submitted, and, sullenly and resentfully, accepted the dictator's promotion system. Two years later, the Artillery Corps was dissolved by royal decree and its officers were not returned to service until after Primo's fall from power, when General Dámaso Berenguer's amnesty of February 18, 1930, restored them to duty.

In January 1929, a leader of the Conservative Party, José Sánchez-Guerra, returned from self-imposed exile in Paris to lead an uprising of artillery officers, centered in Valencia. The movement had a temporary local success in Ciudad Real where the First Light Artillery Regiment seized the city. Elsewhere the revolt fizzled, especially in Valencia, when the Captain General of the Third Military Region, General Alberto Castro-Girona, changed his mind at the last moment and refused to support the movement. Sánchez-Guerra refused to flee, and said with a certain dignity, "I came here to stage a drama, not a farce." He was tried in October 1929, but the court exonerated him. This acquittal was a serious blow to the prestige of the dictatorship.

32

Primo de Rivera suffered from diabetes; also he was sick at heart because of conspirators' inhumanity to dictators. So, when he heard of a new plot against him, late in 1929, he decided to ask for a "vote of confidence". [15] For such a "vote" he could not have recourse to the Cortes, defunct since 1923, nor to the dubiously extra-legal and purely consultative National Assembly; neither could a national plebiscite be organized to vote "*Ja*" in time to prevent or undermine the Andalusian coup which was scheduled to come off not later than February 15, 1930.

Instead, Don Miguel's simple, literal, military mind led him to ask for a "vote of confidence" from the high-ranking military and naval officers, upon whose support he had relied. On January 26, 1930, Primo de Rivera sent out a circular letter to the Captains General and other high officers of the Army and Navy stating that, since it was the military who had set him up as dictator, they should now declare whether he had their confidence and should continue in power. If their replies showed that he no longer had their trust and confidence, Primo promised to step down from power "within five minutes." [16] The response was startling. The generals declared their loyalty to king and country but none proffered protestations of adhesion to the dictator and his régime.

Spain realized that the dictator was through. Two days later, Primo presented to the King his personal resignation together with that of his government. Many thoughtful Spaniards were, of course, angry and resentful after six years of unconstitutional mis-, mal-, and non-feasance under an arbitrary military rule that had become corrupt as well as stupid. But, for most Spaniards of that time, Primo's procedure was scandalous and outrageous because he had ignored the King. By royal prerogative, the Spanish Monarch might represent and speak for the entire nation. And, besides, if General Primo de Rivera wanted to consult the military, he should have done so by addressing himself not to his peers but to his military superior, King Alfonso XIII, Supreme Chief of Defense by Land and Sea.

The six years three and one-half months of Primo de Rivera's dictatorship ended on January 28, 1930, and that same evening King Alfonso entrusted General Dámaso Berenguer with the formation of a Ministry which might serve as a régime of gradual transition to constitutionality. Thus began the *mild* or *soft* "Dicta-*blanda*", in which Spanish punsters saw a marked contrast with the "Dicta-*dura*" of Primo de Rivera. Fifteen turbulent months later, on April 14, 1931, came the second Spanish Republic. The oligarchy had failed, at least temporarily, in its attempt to save the Monarchy and itself by sacrificing the dictator.

As for General Primo de Rivera, he left Madrid on February 12, 1930, stopped off in Barcelona, where he tried unsuccessfully to prevail upon Captain General Emilio Barrera of the IVth Military District to support him in a new military coup, designed to save Spain again, by overthrowing General Berenguer's government. Receiving no encouragement from General Barrera, Primo went on to Paris, where he died on March 16, 1930.

PART TWO

THE APOLITICAL DILEMMA

VI. An Era of Good Feeling

To recapitulate briefly: When Primo came to power in September 1923, he was confronted with a number of national problems inherited from the recent past. Eight of these he considered major and urgent:

1) terrorism and gangsterism,
2) the prevalence of anarchist and communist propaganda,
3) labor unrest,
4) regional separatism,
5) reverses in the Moroccan war,
6) responsibilities for these reverses,
7) bureaucratic inefficiency and waste, and
8) boss rule and corrupt and futile parliamentarism.

That he solved or, at any rate, seemed to solve these prob-lems in an expeditious manner was in large measure due to a happy combination of his own good luck and the good will of large elements among the Spanish people. Indeed, the first months were a veritable honeymoon. A majority among the Spanish people seemed to see in the dictator that "surgeon of iron" so ardently yearned for by Joaquín Costa at the close of the nineteenth century. [17]

Spaniards of nearly all political complexions seemed to be eager to give the General the benefit of every doubt. To a great degree, of course, optimism and hope were born of a desire to escape from feelings of futility and frustration. For example, Manuel García-Prieto, premier of the ministry in power at the time of the coup of September 13, 1923, said with evident relief: "Now I have one more saint to whom to commend myself, Saint Michael Primo de Rivera, because he has taken from me the nightmare of government." [18]

The outstanding leader of the Liberal Party, the Count of Romanones, stated: "Public opinion does well to accept the *coup d'état* with friendly satisfaction, because it understands that that movement frees the country from the inertia of the civil governments." The liberal Madrid daily, *El Sol*, regretted that the change had not taken place half a dozen years earlier. And the then liberal intellectual, José Ortega y Gasset, in the same newspaper, refers to the Military Directory as "those magnanimous generals who, generously and disinterestedly, have realized the half-century-old aspiration of twenty million Spaniards, without its costing the Spanish people any effort whatsoever." [19]

Even more surprising was the political naiveté displayed by two men who later held important positions in the government of the Spanish Republic. The distinguished jurisconsult, diplomatist, and statesman, Angel Ossorio-Gallardo, fixing his attention too closely upon the meaningless and corrupt alternation in power of the "Liberal" and "Conservative" parties, said,

> When the insurgents boast of having given expression to the desires of the people, they are right. Deep in the consciousness of each citizen there blooms a flower of gratitude to those who have interrupted the rotation of greeds (*concupiscencias*).

Niceto Alcalá Zamora, the liberal Catholic constitutional monarchist, who later became a republican, and, finally, the first President of the Spanish Republic, declared:

Let the General be assured of my sincere and cordial desire that this régime (with whose planning and establishing I am in no way connected) may accomplish a mission which will encounter no obstacles on my part.

It seemed that only far to the right and well to the left was there sufficient perspicacity and political realism to permit a correct appraisal of the situation. The conservative leader, José Sánchez-Guerra, prophesied "terrible misfortunes," [20] and General Gonzalo Queipo de Llano, later Generalissimo Franco's most distinguished radio general, said, "They're giving power to Miguel Primo! He will bring us anarchy!" The Socialist party, under the leadership of Indalecio Prieto, declared: "That which Spain repudiates is, apparently, what the seditious generals wish to impose . . . The people, therefore, should not aid them." [21]

This "era of good feeling" was to be short lived. In addition to the ill-will caused by the drastic and makeshift remedies applied by the dictatorship, there were also new sources of dissatisfaction which arose almost inevitably because of the mere existence of the new type of rule in Spain.

Like any new régime, Primo de Rivera's government was concerned with such facts of political life as: 1) accession to power, 2) duration of rule, 3) maintenance of authority, and 4) termination of rule and transmission of the direction of affairs to a successor.

At first, if Primo's rule was to be merely a military occupation of Spain by the Spanish Army, questions of illegality and unconstitutionality could be brushed aside by reference to the unwritten constitution, *la constitución interna,* and to the royal prerogative of the amiable monarch. When, however, it became evident that the dictatorship would rule the country for some time, then the words accession to power, as well as duration, maintenance, and orderly continuity of rule came to represent not mere technicalities but serious problems. Added difficulties were inherent in the fact that Primo's *Putsch* had left much governmental machinery dismantled and unmanned. It at once became necessary to improvise agencies and instruments of government as well as to extemporize policies foreign and domestic.

VII. Problems and Difficulties

1. PREPARATION

WE now turn to problems and difficulties inevitably inherent in or created by the dictatorship. First, let us ask:

What training, preparation, experience, did the dictator bring to his new task?

Practically none, as the General himself freely and proudly admitted. For, although Primo de Rivera failed to realize that the prejudices characteristic of a man of his class and profession should have disqualified him as the ruler of a modern state, he was, in fact, conscious of a lack of technical preparation for the role he had assumed. Of himself and his military colleagues, he said in October 1925, "We had better intentions than preparation."[22] And a few months earlier, when addressing the Somatén militia in Zaragoza, he frankly confessed,

> At times I feel bitterness, because I realize my responsibility, and I bow before the altar of the Fatherland with remorse at not having employed my youth to better advantage... in the necessary technical and cultural preparation which would make my success certain.[23]

But he added that life and experience in commanding soldiers had given him the requisite ability to direct affairs.

41

In March of the same year, 1924, he had told the Association of Catholic Students:

> I have not had experience in governing. Our means are as simple as they are ingenuous. They are the means dictated by the welfare of the Fatherland, and our decisions are taken while we kneel in the sanctuary of the national soul. [24]

The General's admirers had a word for such mystic inspiration: they called it "intuitionism" (*intuicismo, intuicionismo*). [25]

For an evaluation of the results of Primo's *intuicismo,* let us turn to the words of an experienced and intelligent constitutional monarchist, Gabriel Maura-Gamazo, who long collaborated with the dictator and only broke with the régime in 1929, when he realized that Primo had no intention of letting the country return to parliamentary rule under a Cortes. Mr. Maura says:

> But *intuicismo,* like dictatorship, its legitimate daughter, cannot develop into a system of government, because it is justified only occasionally, and is, only under special circumstances, advantageous for the common welfare. [26]

Later he adds:

> There was reflected in the entire work of the dictatorship the innate incapability of *intuicismo* for correct solution of complex general problems. The oversimplified and almost instantaneous solution, maintained with not always praiseworthy stubborn firmness, was bound to restrict itself to but one aspect of the matter, which was never the only one, and sometimes not the most important one either. When the nature of the issue or the way in which it arose did not admit of governmental improvisation, especially as mature experience and cruel failure broke or dented the too optimistic pragmatism of the dictator, it frequently came to pass that perplexity paralyzed his declared purpose for weeks and even whole months, until time, that irreconcilable foe of all inertia, obliged him to act, by now without confidence, too late, and harmfully. [27]

42

Under a parliamentary system, political manipulation and horse trading frequently bring into the cabinet ministers who have little technical background to entitle them to the portfolios assigned to them. Such cabinet ministers may still acquit themselves well in both policy formation and administration if they have a reasonably competent permanent staff of under-secretaries and a secretariat not too much demoralized by a "spoils system." But Primo de Rivera's conscientiously thorough-going housecleaning discredited all bureaucratic functionaries, when it did not abolish their positions entirely. Banished from public life were all "politicians," that is, all those who had had experience in operating either govern-mental or party machinery. The functions of the despised and banished politicos were taken over by army and naval officers. For those, the exhilaration of directing affairs faded when they realized that they were serving as those "bureaucrats" whom they had been taught to despise and when they learned by sad experience that the consecrated phrase "and that's an order!" cannot solve all social and economic problems.

2. TENURE

Let us consider another seemingly innocent question and its complicated answer:

How long was the dictatorship to retain power?

Implicit in this question was a second query: What was the essential nature of the régime?

(a) Was it a short-term caretaker and housecleaning govern-ment? Or (b) was the military occupation of Spain to en-dure as the political expression of a new way of life, like the Fascismo which had just taken over in Italy?

As Don Miguel groped his way along through the years, his answers varied greatly, but his self-assigned term of office tended to lengthen. In September 1923, he not only referred to his assumption of power as acceptance of a 90 day draft, but even asserted that he could accomplish his mission in a much shorter period.

On September 15, 1923, Primo announced the formation of his Military Directory, and added:

> This organism will function for a few days, three weeks, two weeks, thirty days, as long as may be necessary; in short, until the country provides, for the governing of the state, men of the requisite capacity, probity, and will-power. This Directory will busy itself with the function of governing, without the appointment of ministers.
>
> We do not wish to govern. The country will provide the government formed by those persons whom it may consider best qualified to direct all of us and work for the welfare of Spain. [28]

Under the same date, addressing the King in the preamble to the royal decree setting up the Directory, the General had written:

> But Your Majesty well knows that neither I nor those who with me have advocated and proclaimed the new regime believe ourselves qualified for the actual exercise of ministerial posts, and that it was, and continues to be, our purpose to constitute a brief parenthesis in the constitutional development of Spain, in order to reestablish constitutional rule as soon as we can offer to Your Majesty, for the reestablishment of normality, men not contaminated by the vices which we impute to the political organizations. Therefore, I permit myself to offer to YourMajesty the formation of a Military Directory headed by me... etc., etc. [29]

The same theme was recurrent throughout 1924 and 1925, but the time was now indefinite. "I do not know how long we shall remain; as long as it is necessary to save Spain by turning the government over to able persons." [30] The dictator used similar phraseology in addressing the Somatén militia in Zaragoza on May 26th of the same year. By 1925, the dictatorship still had much urgent unfinished business to which to attend, but Primo hoped soon to be be able to turn over power to the Unión Patriótica, his own "non-political" party. [31]

Whether Primo de Rivera really wished to step down from power we can only surmise; but that such an act would have been well received on the second anniversary of the Barcelona coup, we can hardly doubt. Under date of February 11, 1925, the elder statesman and conservative constitutional monarchist, Antonio Maura, wrote the King suggesting transition back to constitutional government. He proposed that the Spaniards' interest in their own government be reawakened by a sampling of public opinion by means of a political questionnaire addressed to such non- or a-political organizations as professional, cultural, economic, agricultural, industrial, and employers' associations, as well as labor unions. [32] How "organic democracy," finding expression in this way, could become effective was not made clear. Alfonso merely acknowledged receipt of this letter from Don Antonio Maura, but on December 2, 1925, His Majesty, in a communication accepting Primo's Ministerial Dictatorship of civilians as successor to the Military Directory, added:

> And I hope that, within a fitting period of time, which I desire may be brief, the country may have laws which set up and establish its normality, and that it may very soon live within a constitutional framework, in order that it may no longer need a period of emergency rule. [33]

With the year 1925 ended the ingenuous, optimistic, housecleaning aspect of Primo's rule. During the term of the "90-day draft" of 1923, the naive Don Miguel had actually hoped and expected to turn the government over to a body of patriotic civilians, uncontaminated by any previous involvement in vile politics. When it became evident that no such holy innocents

45

were likely to be found, the General and his associates were delighted to have the opportunity to demonstrate to all Spaniards and to the world that it was the military who really knew how to run a state and its government—and all without politics!

Martial law, proclaimed on September 15, 1923, was ended on May 16, 1925. On September 8, 1925, General Primo de Rivera directed the fortunate amphibious operation which resulted in capture of Alhucemas in Morocco, which was the beginning of the end for Abd-El-Krim. If the dictator had stepped down in December 1925, he would no doubt have been remembered as the savior of his land and people. Unfortunately for him and for Spain, he did not realize that the honeymoon had long been over, that the people were becoming restive and the Army disaffected, as a result of the frustrations incident to the necessity of undertaking unfamiliar tasks for which it was ill-prepared. Mounting opposition became more bitter and implacable because of Primo's stubborn meddlesomeness and, as a result, it became practically impossible for him to relinquish power, although he still insisted that such was his desire. [34]

On the last day of 1929, disheartened by his difficulties with the army officers and the military conspiracies against his régime, as well as by the decline of the peseta, Don Miguel proposed still another transition government which was to last three years, but His Majesty, probably realizing that the end was in sight, was noncommittal in his response to the suggestion. [35]

And finally, a few days before his fall, Primo hinted that he might retire from power on September 13, 1930, the seventh anniversary of the Barcelona coup. Instead, he was forced out of power on January 28, 1930, thus ending the career of a dictator who had overstayed his welcome by some four or five years.

Nevertheless, as he was leaving for Paris on February 12, 1930, Primo is reported to have said that Spain would have to remain under a dictatorship until

> new generations make it possible to give to the country a more civic and liberal structure, because one must confess that, up to now, true liberty—that liberty which guarantees property, life, decency, and tranquillity—must be accompanied by Civil Guards.[36]

3. STATUS

There was a third question, which one might have expected a military dictatorship to treat with derision and contempt. But such was not the case. Neither the General nor his opposition considered this matter at all irrelevant or academic:

What was the moral, legal, and constitutional status of the régime?

In other words, wasn't the dictatorship conceived in treason and born of mutiny and lawlessness? To leave this question unanswered might have very serious practical consequences for the mutinous generals and their collaborators. Two most important aspects were the violation of the officers' oath of loyalty to the constitutional monarchy as both fact and precedent, and the attitude of the dictatorship with regard to the Constitution of 1876.

Primo referred to the Barcelona coup as the "illegal but patriotic act of September 13." [37] He also termed it "a violation of discipline, which is the true sacrament of the Army." But, in justification of his coup, he continued: "That day, we considered that discipline was secondary in comparison with the immense good which we could bestow upon the Fatherland." [38]

47

In fact, in his original pronunciamiento of September 12, 1923, in Barcelona, Primo had made a similar appeal:

> We have not conspired. We have, in broad daylight, championed the aspirations of the people and we have given them something in the way of organization, in order to direct them toward a patriotic end devoid of ambitions.
>
> Although we may come into being through an act of technical indiscipline, we do represent that true discipline, which is due our principles and love of country, and so we shall conceive, practice, and require discipline, not forgetting that since we are not moved by ambition but, on the contrary, by the spirit of sacrifice, ours is the highest authority.[39]

However, the General was not unmindful of the possibility that some other equally patriotic officer might wish to imitate him and save the Fatherland all over again. Hence, Primo devoted great pains and emphasis to preaching "union." *La unión* meant disciplined unity and harmony of the officer corps of the several arms and the Navy.

His theme was that "the union of the entire Army is necessary for its strength, which is the support for national strength." [40]

He had, since his days as a cadet, opposed the *Juntas de Defensa,* officers' associations of the different arms and services. "The *Juntas,* an expression of ill-being, tended to disunite us. Now there is a holy union, without any break in discipline." [41]

As a matter of fact, the factional strife within the Army did not develop as Primo had feared. The plotting of the officers was, in the main, directed against him personally. And there was among the Captains General unanimity, if not union, when they caused the dictator's fall from power by refusing him a vote of confidence, on January 26, 1930.

The Spanish Constitution of 1876, which provided for responsible parliamentary government under a limited monarchy had, in fact, been overthrown by Primo's Barcelona coup of September 13, 1923, but the official version was that it had only been suspended pending the return of normality. Indeed, that Constitution of 1876 was cherished with much of the reverence due a holy relic captured from the enemy. This feeling of almost superstitious awe was, no doubt, reinforced in the dictator's mind by the very practical consideration that he did not want any rival to raise the dead constitution as a standard of revolt.

On several occasions the dictator stated that the one basic prerequisite for membership in his apolitical *Unión Patriótica* was that the potential member should accept and respect the Constitution of 1876. For example, on the 15th of April 1924, he said in a statement to the press in Barcelona: "There is room in the party for all those who revere the Constitution of 1876." Again, in a speech on August 21 of the same year, Primo said of his "Patriotic Union" that it

should be made up of all those who accept the Constitution of 1876. That is to say, of all those who accept and revere the precepts contained in the fundamental code of the nation.[42]

By the end of his third year as dictator, Primo would preserve the old Constitution only until his newly created (and entirely unconstitutional!) National Assembly should be able to frame new fundamental laws. The dictatorship, he says,

continues its evolution toward a normality which is not to be exactly that of the past, but the most perfect which can be offered to the country without prejudgment or anulment of the constitutional law, center and soul of public life, so long as it may not be modified legally.[43]

On March 6, 1928, in an address commemorating the centenary of the birth of Antonio Cánovas del Castillo, under whose conservative leadership the Constitution of 1876 was promulgated, Primo de Rivera declared that new problems of the day, such as communism, regional separatism, and the lack of social cohesion, made that constitution unsuitable for Spain in 1928, and added that the great Cánovas, if he were still alive, would "tear up his work, considering it inadequate, inefficacious, and too valetudinarian to protect society from new attacks and dangers." [44]

By the end of the year 1929, the change in the dictator's attitude toward the Constitution was complete. During that year a committee of the National Assembly had produced the first draft of a new constitution. [45] Primo intended to have it discussed, amended, and approved by the largely appointed National Assembly before offering it as a new constitution to the citizenry at large by means of a plebiscite to be held in 1930. Hence, in his press release of New Year's Day 1930, he referred to the old Constitution of 1876 as *aquel artilugio,* "that contraption." [46]

In February 1930, even after he had fallen from power and was about to leave Madrid, the General was still preoccupied by the problem of the "legality and constitutionality" of his next coup, which he fatuously expected to occur as soon as he should reach Barcelona. According to his worshipful admirer, Eduardo Aunós, the General referred first to past need for a constitution, saying: "We should have drawn one up before anything else; our former procedure was exactly the reverse of what the circumstances required." But, he said,

this time I shall not be caught off guard. I am going to incite the Barcelona garrison to mutiny; but I shall take along with me in my pocket a constitution which I shall immediately have submitted to a vote of the people and I shall exact strict responsibility from each of the organs of the State, from the highest to the lowest. (*Primo de Rivera,* p. 222).

Unable to win the support of the Captain General of Barcelona, Primo took the next train for Paris. Although Spain is said to be the land in which public affairs are usually conducted in a manner completely opposed to the constitutional way of doing things—*anticonstitucionalísimamente,* as the Spanish wits have it—Primo de Rivera's nineteenth century standards of parliamentary legality would not permit him to share the cynical impartiality and the ignorant serenity of such dictators as the Bolivian Colonel Mariano Melgarejo, who once declared, at a banquet:

> "I want the gentleman who has just spoken and all the honorable deputies gathered here to know that I have put the Constitution of 1861, which was very good, in this pocket (pointing to his left trouser pocket) and that of 1868, which is even better in the opinion of these gentlemen, in this one (pointing to his right pocket) and that nobody is going to rule in Bolivia but me." [47]

4. SURVIVAL

How was Primo's régime to maintain itself in power?

What of "law and order"? Would the Army, the constabulary, and the security service suffice? And then, who would maintain order in the Army and who would police the police?

Again, would it be possible to eliminate "politics" by decree, and forbid all opposition whether loyal or subversive? What would be the final effect if such a political vacuum could be created? The dictator's attempts to answer such questions were bound to be interesting and instructive.

Primo de Rivera sought to preserve the "police potential" of the Army by limiting to the very highest echelons the opportunities for indiscipline, mutiny and treason. The coup of 1923 was plotted among generals and admirals because it would have been impossible to take into consultation the lower ranks and grades "without loosening the bonds of discipline." [48] On January 26, 1930, the circular letter to the captains general, in which Primo asked for a "vote of confidence" urged that these

51

high-ranking officers should give him their opinion after a "brief, discreet, and confidential investigation, which must not go lower than the commanding officers of units and services." [49] And, as we have noted above, throughout the period 1923-1930, Primo harped again and again on the theme of "union" of the armed forces, which to him meant loyalty and obedience to the dictator.

Primo's simple military habits of thought usually caused him to assume that his own "intuitional" solution to a problem was the only one possible. His positive interventionism caused him many difficulties. He was likely to compound state interventionism with his own impulsive personal meddling in administrative and legal matters.

Let the following episode serve as an example of Primo's personal rule. In 1924, "La Caoba" (The Mahogany Girl) was being prosecuted in a Madrid court by the sons of a protector or patron of hers. Primo wrote for her a letter of recommendation to Judge Prendes Pando. The magistrate not only rejected the "fix," but insisted on introducing the letter into the official court records of the case. When Chief Justice Buenaventura Muñoz of the Supreme Court refused to discipline Judge Prendes Pando, Primo forced the resignation of the Chief Justice and had the stubborn Judge transferred to Oviedo in northern Spain.

Satirical references to the episode, in a speech in the Madrid Ateneo by a Valencian republican, Rodrigo Soriano, caused the speaker to be exiled to Fuerteventura in the Canary Islands. Miguel de Unamuno, essayist, novelist, and professor of Greek at the University of Salamanca, wrote to a friend in Buenos Aires, making sarcastic reference to this same incident. The letter was published in Argentina and Unamuno was also exiled to Fuerteventura. Professor García del Real, of the Madrid Faculty of Medicine, and Law Professors Fernando de los Ríos and Luis Jiménez de Asúa were subjected to court action for protesting against the decree exiling Unamuno, and Jiménez de Asúa was himself exiled to the Chafarinas Islands, off the coast of northeast Morocco.

Unamuno was deprived of his professorship but, with the help of French friends, went to Paris and then on to Hendaye, whence he and others waged a propaganda war against the dictatorship. In Spain, as time went on, many professors resigned their chairs, but the University of Salamanca, far from protesting against the illegal dismissal of its distinguished professor of Greek, actually conferred upon General Primo de Rivera the degree of doctor *honoris causa!*

Six years later, with Unamuno still in exile, the University of Valladolid showed its disapproval of the dictatorship by electing to Primo's brand new and extra-constitutional National Consultative Assembly none other than Don Miguel de Unamuno! Angrily, the Cabinet, on October 6, 1929, annulled that election, adding: "Unamuno never was a professor at the University of Valladolid and now he is no professor at all." [50]

Frequent student riots still further exasperated the general. Even more painful to him personally was the fact that literary men detested his censorship and made sport of his own prose style, for the dictator considered himself a literary artist, and his verbose, pompous and rhetorical prose was an inviting target for the sarcastic shafts of the intellectuals.

Little openly expressed opposition to the régime came from the discredited políticos and their parties or from organized labor, for the politicians had been cowed and the General Labor Union, the UGT, had been taken into partnership by Don Miguel.

The most active opposition came from two unlike and antagonistic sources: from the Army and from the intellectuals. Among the latter, authors and journalists were annoyed by Primo's censorship, and students and professors resented the dictator's arbitrary intervention in university affairs. The dictator's tendency to meddle in the business of the courts was also resented.

The fact is that, despite a veneer of sophistication and slight "contamination" by liberal patterns and ideas, Don Miguel's ideal was the irresponsibly benevolent oriental despot. As Mr. Madariaga says, "Even though his conscious ideal may have been Signor Mussolini (which is by no means certain) his subconscious model would rather be Haroun al Raschid." [51] His Jehovah complex led him to take delight in waiving regulations, commuting sentences, and imposing arbitrary and illegal fines.

Primo de Rivera's mind could not conceive toleration of organized political opposition or of an uncensored press. In his opinion, nobody had "the right to be wrong." One year after Primo had assumed power, the presidents of the Spanish press associations requested that pre-publication censorship be lifted, but the general refused, saying,

> The right to promote one theory or another is a piece of simplicity tolerated only in a period of decadence. Governments have the duty of manipulating all means and resources of national activity, in that cadence which they consider beneficial to the country and society which they are directing. [52]

At that time he hoped to enact a press code "to make the press be good," adding that, "A good newspaper is more useful and efficacious than six schools; a bad paper will do more damage than a cyclone." [53]

Four years later he had not changed his opinion at all. The press must be watched and controlled by the government in order that it might foster good citizenship instead of being an instrumentality of politics; for,

> Who would permit the daily entrance into his home of a preacher and agitator who might inculcate prematurely in his children inadequate anxieties and suspicions and might irresponsibly overthrow values which we judge indispensable to the order and the life of the society which we have established? Well, that's what a newspaper usually is. [54]

54

Primo insisted upon "previous censorship," i. e., the galleys had to be sent to the censor for approval and returned, before the edition could be printed. The censor's okeh was ordinarily considered as giving immunity from fine or suspension after publication, but this principle, too, was at times honored in the breach. Ordinarily, editors live in fear of prosecution for what they print. It remained for Primo de Rivera to fine *La Epoca* of Madrid for an omission, despite his censor's okeh.

The sequence of events was as follows: in October 1925, King Alfonso conferred upon General Primo de Rivera the high military decoration known as the Cross of San Fernando. The ceremony took place in the royal palace and was publicized in the Madrid press. In January 1926, Major Ramón Franco, the brother of the present Spanish dictator, returned in triumph from his flight to Buenos Aires. [55] An appropriate celebration of this event was held at the Cuatro Vientos airport. In order to get into the act, and shine in reflected glory, the dictator childishly insisted on re-enacting the conferral of his decoration. *La Epoca* took the position that Don Miguel's October cross was no longer news, made no mention whatsoever of Primo's presence at the event, but did carry a full report of the ceremony honoring Major Franco, which was duly passed by the censor. The slight was, no doubt, deliberate, and Primo was not the man to brook such contumely. Since he too could say, "I am the law," it was no trouble for him to maintain his contention that failure to print "important" news was actionable and that the fact that the censor had approved the news story with the insulting omission made no difference. *La Epoca* was at first fined 25,000 pesetas, later reduced by one-half, that is, to about two thousand dollars. [56]

VIII. Apolitical Politics

O N July 31, 1928, Don Miguel spoke of politics as compounded of "corruption and violence," under the title: "The past has departed to return no more." On this ocasion he said:

> Therefore, we do not want to engage in politics, because that sort of thing is old fashioned and inadequate and because there has already been created for the civilization of the world a state of law, a juridical situation based upon that which alone is indisputable and true, which is the teaching of Christ.
> There has been created a juridical state, and, therefore, to speak of politics comes to be somewhat incomprehensible.[57]

From this attitude it is but a short and easy step to the conviction that all politics and all politicians are by definition evil. It was "politics, damned politics," said Primo, which was the destruction of Spain and which then (1929) was seeking to undo all the good work of the dictatorship. Politics was a poison and the enemy of the people. [58]

By politics Primo understood, of course, the corrupt parliamentarism and the caricature of representative democracy which had been misgoverning Spain for a full century. From this he generalized, holding that no ministerial cabinet responsible to a parliament could be either just or efficacious. On the other hand, Primo spoke with pride of his apolitical régime; on February 18, 1929, he declared with satisfaction:

Five and one-half years of one single government without holding elections have extinguished the partisan and personalist political measles from which the country suffered, and have rejuvenated and purified its blood, through which now circulate red corpuscles and not toxins.[59]

Primo de Rivera did, however, have an instinctive understanding of his régime's need for social cohesion and mass support. He also realized that his trade union backing might well be counter-balanced by an organization designed to attract support from the middle and propertied classes. Accordingly, he set up a *Unión Patriótica*. During the six years of his rule, Primo again and again defined his Patriotic Union and explained over and over again, but not always with consistency, the role of this "apolitical party" in the development of the new Spain. [60]

Primo de Rivera held that there were but two types of Spaniards: low-lived political bosses and their bólivars and ward-heelers, on the one hand, and pure, high-minded patriots on the other. The military coup had turned the rascals out, ostracised them, and dissolved their parties. Military officers were substituting for them in government positions. Primo still hoped to turn power and authority over to men who had not governed before, and who would rule in accordance with his ideas.[61] He thought that the only way to save Spain from a Tweedledum-Tweedledee alternation of parties, from frustrating parliamentarism, and from greedy politicians and boss rule was to call to office and to power a vast company of holy apolitical innocents and noble neutrals, a civic militia of high-minded *Cincinnati* who would rush from their plows and counting-houses able and eager to do just what the General thought he wanted them to do. The dictator was, of course, astonished and dismayed to find that most of the neutrals remained neutral and that few of the innocents were politically employable.

58

According to Primo the *Unión Patriótica* was not a party but *una conducta organizada,* a way of life. He also characterized the U.P. as a retaining wall or barricade erected to hold back the rubble of the political structure which the coup had overthrown. Again, it is a league, a consortium, and the one-and-only Spanish party. Soon, it was an association of men of good faith, apolitical or political, "who have not been contaminated by past vices and who are widely known to be worthy." [62]

The party's mission was to set an example of civic spirit, to provide personnel for government, to create a government worthy of the dictatorship. The Patriotic Union and its leaders would be qualified to rule precisely because it and they did not wish to govern. [63]

At first all applicants for U.P. membership were required to "accept the Constitution of 1876," that is, they must support the constitutional monarchy. Later, "There is room in the Patriotic Union for all men of good will and that without their forsaking their convictions. Even those who are not monarchists, provided they respect the person of the Chief of State, may find a place in these ranks." [64] At times the party was represented as being neutral, as between right and left. Again, its ideology was eclectic. "Its program is most ample, and derives from rightist as well as left ideologies, provided they offer possible benefits for the country." [65]

Let us conclude our discussion of the theory of the Patriotic Union by quoting from its *Cartilla,* or "Primer," and its *Decálogo*: [66]

What is the Patriotic Union?

The Patriotic Union is a grouping of Spaniards who undertake to be outstanding in the fulfillment of their duties.

Which are the political duties?

59

The defense of the Monarchy. Respectful submission to authority and discipline. Voting in elections to public office. Personal intervention in the maintenance of order. The acceptance and proper discharge of public offices to which one may be appointed. Vigilance in the carrying out of the laws.

What is the origin of the Patriotic Union?

The holy rebellion of the military uprising which, under orders of General Primo de Rivera, saved Spain from imminent ruin.

Is the Patriotic Union a political party?

It is not a political party; it is a civic organization with the objective of maintaining a program, together with persons who incarnate and defend that program, availing itself of the political elections which may be held and watching over the fulfillment of the aforementioned duties.

And from the "Decalogue":

I. I detest all sectarian or partisan politics because I wish to serve my fatherland with a comprehensive ideology and personal independence, without owing to any influence which represents favoritism the justice which is mine by right.

In August 1927, there was a suggestion that Primo might be thinking in terms of a monolithic party-state. The Patriotic Union was not, he said, a political party; it was rather a citizens' crusade of purification and regeneration, *una cruzada civil saneadora*. Primo's further remarks indicate that, for him, the *Unión Patriótica* was the only true Spain and that, therefore, its scope, responsibilities, and powers must be greater than those of any merely political organization:

Since the Patriotic Union. . . is not a party but rather an organized way of life, a posture adopted in view of the nation's circumstances, there is no reason why it should tolerate differences of opinion and partisan strife. . . Hence the Patriotic Union does not have a press of its own, nor does it recognize the existence of any opposition; it is, we repeat, the assemblage of men of all convictions, who meet and

60

organize, impelled by their consciences, in order to purify and exalt politics... Its program is truly comprehensive and is based upon ideologies of both the right and the left, provided they represent possible advantages for the country. This means an enormous progress in policy, which has not been understood by all, and is what gives the party an apolitical nature which permits us to assign to the Patriotic Unions a more official and state character than doctrinaire and personalist parties could ever have.[67]

Primo de Rivera said repeatedly that the Patriotic Union must not monopolize government jobs and appointments. It must "train and point out" good men who would make competent public servants. [68] For the régime was to make judicial, administrative, and technical appointments from the entire citizenry, not from the party alone.

At other times, the General got down to a few grass-root realities. The cabinet ministers must remain impartial and therefore could not hold office in local or provincial branches of the Patriotic Union.

He held that the civil governors of the provinces need not necessarily be members of the party, and that they should not be appointed by the provincial *Unión Patriótica*. However, there should be a majority of U. P. members in the provincial legislatures and on the township boards. And when the "civil" governor, who was often an army or naval officer, had to make an appointment, he was, if possible, to make his selection from three names to be suggested to him by the local party organization. [69] These measures, as well as occasional purges and expulsions from the party, indicated an intention on Primo's part to prevent the development of local machines and bosses, which might destroy party discipline, and to prevent clashes between the little big shots of the party and the proud and contemptuous army officers. They also indicated that Primo was still trying to attract into the party new members of some social standing.

In assessing the social usefulness of the Patriotic Union, we shall first note the verdicts of men closely associated with the dictator.

Eduardo Aunós was a civilian Minister of Labor in Primo's Ministerial Dictatorship, as well as a great admirer of the General; after the Spanish Civil War he became Generalissimo Franco's Minister of Grace and Justice. Writing a dozen years after his hero's fall from power, Mr. Aunós declared that Primo's attempt to banish all politicians and parties, and to set up in their place a new all-inclusive apolitical organization was to undertake the impossible, in view of the fact that the dictator's situation and prejudices deprived the new patriotic monopoly of prestige, tradition, personnel, and know-how. Most of those "righteous, learned, industrious, and upright men" whom the dictator sought to recruit into the Patriotic Union were already contaminated by their former participation in parliamentary politics and must therefore be "ostracised," as Primo was fond of saying. What really happened, says Mr. Aunós, was that the most active elements in the new Patriotic Union were drawn from would-be politicos who had been unsuccessful in their attempts to rise to leadership in the old parties, as well as nimble band-wagon jumpers of similar origin. [70]

Gabriel Maura-Gamazo, an optimistic and unhappy constitutional monarchist who collaborated with the dictatorship until 1929, was more specific and definite in characterizing the elements attracted to the *Unión Patriótica*. The party was, he says, "an inconsistent mixture of three heterogeneous groups." These three groups were: (a) the Carlists, pro-clerical absolute monarchists; (b) those who represented special interests with an economic axe to grind; and (c) the local bosses and their henchmen, who were so conditioned that they easily rose above ideologies in order to pounce upon patronage and plunder.

62

Of the conflicting demands of the members of the second group, Mr. Maura says:

In the U. P. there enrolled, then, persons of widely differing political convictions, convictions which they laid aside in order to have, as supporters of the régime, more satisfactory dealings with the government: low prices for those who were consumers, high prices for producers; limitation of imports for those who supplied the Spanish market, encouragement of exports for those who sold abroad; protection of industry for manufacturers, protection of agricultural products for farmers; hard money for some merchants who buy their stocks abroad, favorable exchange for others who sell for gold abroad; international (trade) agreements or tariff wars; labor and raw material to be cheap or dear; the system, in short, which best suited the personal convenience of each one.[71]

Mr. Maura adds that the men of the third group, the hardy perennials among the local bosses, in time came to dominate the party, due to the fact that Gresham's law is even more applicable to political than to monetary circulation, and therefore, there came to the surface, in councils, mayors' offices, provincial legislatures, and party headships, the most adroit survivers of the old politics, that is to say, with occasional exceptions, the sucessful were crafty, ambitious, unscrupulous, and parasitic!

In brief, then, we may say that Primo's apolitical venture was a failure. The Patriotic Union failed to recruit a sufficient number of "new men" and it failed to keep out of political circulation the local bosses and politicasters who, Primo thought, were the cause of Spain's social woes. The dictator found it impossible to fill a political vacuum by means of an apolitical monopoly.

IX. Toward Legality: The National Assembly

GENERAL Primo de Rivera declared in 1928 that he held himself responsible for his political measures and his rule "before my conscience and before History" or "before God, Fatherland, and King." [72] Court flatterers, of course, took delight in repeating this trite little compliment. The cultured poet and dramatist, José María Pemán, who is also an apologist of absolute monarchy and an admirer of dictators, bowed, then, before Primo as he now bows before Franco. Addressing the former, he said:

> Nunca os cause desazones
> el inútil murmurar
> de las vanas opiniones;
> que a Dios sólo habéis de dar
> cuenta de vuestras acciones. [73]

Despite such lofty talk, Primo seemed in doubt, at times, as to just what role he should assign to himself and his crusade. In 1923, during the first three months of his rule, the General thought of himself as a short-term house-cleaner and reformer. At the beginning of 1924, he toyed with the idea of developing the Somatén militia into a Spanish Fascio. Throughout 1924 and 1925 it was evident that the régime no longer felt that its rule would be of short duration. The military were in the saddle and eager to show how a government should be run; it was necessary to improvise policy both foreign and domestic.

65

In 1926, the Patriotic Union began to function. The party had already held meetings, banquets, and demonstrations in Madrid, Valladolid, Segovia, Barcelona, Medina del Campo, Santander, in 1923 and 1924, and, in the following year, in Andalusia: Sevilla, Córdoba, Málaga, Jerez. The Madrid daily, *La Nación*, became the official organ of the *Unión Patriótica* on October 19, 1925.

In April 1926, the General declared that, since his government had consultative commissions and technicians, it had no need of elections and parliaments which could only mean "a return to times of shameful boss rule." [74]

Nevertheless, Primo was, in fact, not only concerned about the illegality and unconstitutionality of his régime but also had need of reassurance regarding his popularity with the Spanish people. The Patriotic Union, of which the dictator was president, obligingly asked and received permission to conduct a nation-wide plebiscite on September 11, 12, 13, 1926, to "prove" the universal popularity in Spain of the dictatorship. As was to be expected, the General "won" in the plebiscite. First of all, there was no opportunity for anyone to vote against him. In the second place, the vote was conducted by the Patriotic Union.

In all the provinces of Spain, there were set up, in appropiate places, tables where the citizens could voluntarily and spontaneously leave their signatures. This was the way of indicating their adhesion to the government. Everywhere the success was extraordinary, and great crowds came up to sign, without being coerced in any way. The total number of signers attained the unusual figure of 7,506,488. [75]

Encouraged by such an overwhelming, though rigged, vote of confidence, Primo felt justified in convoking the long-promised and unconstitutional National Assembly. The royal decree of September 12, 1927, set the opening date of the sessions for October 10, 1927. To this body, the term "con-

66

sultative" or "advisory" was frequently applied. Its functions were to be two: (a) it was to investigate, evaluate, and advise concerning the work of the dictatorship during the preceding four years and (b) it was to draw up basic legislation for future consideration by "an elective legislative organ." [76]

So far as constitutional law was concerned, the situation was hopelessly confused because: (a) the dictatorship insisted that the Constitution of 1876 was suspended but not abrogated; but (b) that dictatorship also refused to permit a return to parliamentary rule by cabinets of responsible ministers, as provided in the constitution; and (c) the Constitution of 1876 contained no provision for amendment. The National Assembly consisted of about 400 members, including eleven women. The members held their seats *ex officio* or by election, or through appointment by the dictatorship. Members *ex officio* were the provincial chiefs of the Patriotic Union and the representatives from the important provincial legislatures and township governments, as well as chairmen of governmental boards and commissions *(corporaciones)*. Some of these latter resigned from their commissions rather than serve in the National Assembly.

Since Primo consistently wooed organized labor, he invited both the Socialist Party and the UGT (General Workers Union) to send representatives. Although Francisco Largo-Caballero of the UGT was a labor member of the Council of State, the socialists as a party and the unions followed the leadership of Indalecio Prieto and refused to participate in the National Assembly. [77]

There was also conservative opposition to the calling of the National Assembly. Although José Sánchez-Guerra, as head of the Conservative Party, had himself been responsible for playing a certain amount of low-level politics and although, since 1923, he had swallowed many an unconstitutional dictatorial camel, he now chose to strain at the extra-legal gnat which

67

took the form of a National Assembly. Sánchez-Guerra accordingly declared that the convoking of the unconstitutional National Assembly was an outrage and that he was taking his family into voluntary exile with him to Paris. From there, he returned to Valencia in 1929, to lead a conspiracy against the dictator. [78]

The sessions of the new Assembly were held in the building where the Chamber of Deputies formerly met, but the name plaque now read "Asamblea Nacional" instead of "Congreso de los Diputados." The presiding officer of the National Assembly was not elected by its members but appointed by the dictator; to this office Primo named José Yanguas-Messía, professor of international law at the University of Madrid and former Minister of State (foreign affairs).

King Alfonso XIII attended the opening session of the Assembly on October 10, 1927. The approximately 400 members were divided into eighteen sections or large committees. Section number one devoted itself to the preparation of the first draft of a new constitution. This document, which was completed but never adopted or even fully debated, is known to Spaniards as the *Anteproyecto de Constitución de 1929*.

The first plenary session took place on October 29. General Primo de Rivera was in command and he saw to it that deliberations proceeded "by the numbers" and with parade ground snap and expeditiousness. Three hours were allowed for consideration of each matter. Cabinet ministers were allowed 30 minutes for speeches and 15 minutes for replies, members were permitted 20 minutes for speeches and ten minutes for replies. "A barracks system of deliberation," says Antonio Ballesteros. [79] The Assembly was to convene every year in October and adjourn the following July. The first National Assembly closed its sessions on June 28, 1928.

The eighteen sections devoted themselves to study of matters referred to them by the dictator and his Cabinet.

68

Among these were: tribunals for the protection of citizens, emigration, laws concerning inheritance, agrarian associations, religious instruction, reform of secondary education, and the new constitution mentioned above.

All such matters were studied, reported on, and even discussed, but never came to a vote. Primo would sum up the discussion and express "the sense of the meeting," if it did not conflict with the opinion of the dictator. So far as concerned interpellations from the floor, the calendar was always full and the time limited, and, besides, a minister could always reject any question or interpellation. Moreover, there would not be a vote on the questions, much less a vote of lack of confidence, and the dictator's government could not "fall" anyway. [80]

During the summer of 1929, before the 1929-30 meeting of the National Assembly, the dictator decided to increase the membership of that body in order to make it more representative. This was, no doubt, an excellent idea, especially if the Assembly was to be the instrumentality of transition to legality, constitutionalism, and normalcy. However, Primo found that one can hardly expect the support and cooperation of those whom one has been studiously insulting for six years —in this case the leaders of the much-berated political parties, the intellectuals and certain members of the liberal professions. The eight former premiers and other dignitaries received Primo's offer with contemptuous silence.

The dictator also offered a total of forty-one seats to such "corporations" as the Royal Academies, the universities, the associations of doctors and of lawyers in Madrid and Barcelona, the labor unions, the Association for the League of Nations, etc. He found the response disheartening, not to say infuriating. On September 25, 1929, the Academy of Jurisprudence voted to abstain from being represented in the National Assembly. The University of Valladolid elected as

69

its representative Don Miguel de Unamuno, whom Primo had sent into exile in 1924, and who was then conducting a propaganda campaign against the dictatorship from the French side of the frontier. On October 5, 1929, the Madrid Bar Association duly elected the three delegates to which it was entitled. They were: Santiago Alba, the politician whom Primo detested most heartily of all, and who was an exile in France; Eduardo Ortega-Gasset, another intellectual in exile; and José Sánchez-Guerra, who was at that very moment on trial as leader of the Valencia conspiracy against the dictatorship. [81] In such ways did opposition to Primo's dictatorship manage to express itself.

During the remaining weeks of Don Miguel's rule, the National Assembly languished, and it was finally abolished by royal decree on February 15, 1930, eighteen days after the end of the dictatorship. [82]

X. The Still - Born Constitution of 1929

HAVING declared that the Spanish Constitution of 1876 was antiquated and unusable, the dictator first undertook to amend it. Of the thirteen "Titles" or sections of the Constitution of 1876, Primo contemplated a virtual rewriting of Titles II, III, IV, V, and VI. These amendments seem to have been drawn up by Primo personally and submitted by him to the first section of the National Assembly of 1927-28. A copy was smuggled out of Spain and published in France in the anti-Primo propaganda publication of Miguel de Unamuno and Eduardo Ortega-Gasset, known as *Hojas Libres* (Free Leaves).[83] With only slight changes, most of the 37 articles of Primo's "amendments" were included in the Draft Constitution of 1929.

The 1929 Draft of a New Constitution, *Anteproyecto de Constitución de 1929,* is dated May 17, 1929, and was presented to the National Assembly on July 6th of that year. The text was published in *El Debate* of Madrid on Sunday, July 7, 1929.

Although the draft was largely the work of others, and was also in many respects similar to the Constitution of 1876, it did contain a number of provisions which had long been advocated by Primo de Rivera.

In the first article, Spain was declared to be a unitary state and its government a constitutional monarchy.

71

Reproduced verbatim was Article 11 of the Constitution of 1876, which declared that Catholicism was the state religion. Also, Article 26 of the draft, concerning education, the granting of degrees, and freedom to practice a profession, was taken verbatim from Article 12 of the Constitution of 1876.

Draft Article 104 provided for amendment to the new constitution, a provision which had been omitted (probably deliberately) from the Constitution of 1876.

A few articles undertook to eliminate, at least in theory, some of the more flagrant abuses of the dictatorship. Article 29 forbade prior censorship. Article 63 provided that state monopolies must be specifically authorized by law—(waste and graft had resulted from Primo's arbitrary, and, no doubt, "intuitional" procedure regarding such matters as tobacco, petroleum products, telephones, etcetera). Articles 97-99 forbade executive interference in the administration of justice.

Article 64 forbade the legislature to make permanent transfer to the executive power of its duties and responsibilities.

Among the draft provisions which had had Primo's active support were the following:

1) state and government intervention in education and in the use of private property;

2) a charter of labor's rights, which included state sponsored arbitration; to this end, workers were encouraged, almost required to organize into unions; (84)

3) universal suffrage, with women having the right to vote and hold office—Primo expected the devout Spanish woman to be a stabilizing counter-balance to the "radical" Masonic liberalism of her men folks;

4) in theory, a unicameral legislature was provided to take the place of the old Cortes, which had consisted of a Senate as well as a Congress of Deputies; as a matter of fact, the "Fifth Title" of the draft set up a *Consejo del Reino,* a Council of the

72

Realm, which was invested with most of the powers and attributes of the former Senate;

5) parliamentary responsibility was to be non-existent; the pertinent paragraph of Article 66 read as follows:

> Article 66. The voting by which the Cortes approve or reject bills or other proposals of the Executive Power will not necessarily imply the replacement of the ministers. The Cabinet and the deputies may not propose, nor the Cortes adopt, resolutions which signify political confidence with respect to the members of the Cabinet and other functionaries of the executive.

The general trend of the draft of 1929 was to strengthen the executive, especially by enhancing the royal prerogative until it might almost be said that the monarchy was to be "constitutional" but only slightly "limited." To the monarch were ascribed the following duties and functions: (1) the king was to be the moderator who would maintain the independence and harmony of the separate powers of government (Article 43). (2) "The power of making the laws resides in the Cortes with the king, who will approve and promulgate them." (Art. 43). (3) The Chairman of the Council of the Realm was to be appointed and removed at the pleasure of the king, who would appoint all but nine of the members of the permanent half of the councilors (Articles 44 and 45). After hearing the advice of the Council, the king would appoint a temporary regent when occasion should require, would dissolve the Cortes, or appoint the premier (Art. 48). King and cabinet were to initiate legislation regarding defense, foreign affairs, and (with one exception) finance (Art. 62). King and ministers exercised the executive power (Art. 68). The king might add to the cabinet ministers without portfolio (Art. 69). He approved the list of ministers submitted by a new premier (Art. 69). As chief of the executive the king had fourteen other functions (Art. 70). The fact that José María Pemán, an absolute mon-

73

archist, was secretary of the drafting commission might have had much to do with this aspect of the draft of 1929. For his part, the garrulous and officious dictator, not behind but out in front of the throne, needed a strongly monarchist constitution for reasons of his own. Primo seemed never to have regarded the King as a rival for power. To the General, His Majesty was a symbol, a mascot, a hostage, an unreliable ally, or even a royal nuisance at times, but certainly no rival. *"¡A mí no me borbonea ése!"* said Primo of his royal master on one occasion—"That fellow shan't play any of his dirty Bourbon tricks on me!"

Of political interest is Primo's arbitrary change in the proposed manner of ratifying or rejecting the Draft Constitution of 1929. Sometime between October 1927 and July 1929, the dictator dropped the idea of ratification by Cortes and decided in favor of referendum by plebiscite. On October 10, 1927, the chairman of the first National Assembly, Dr. José Yanguas-Messía, promised, in Primo's presence, that

> drafts of basic legislation prepared by the Assembly will, at the proper time, come up for examination and decision before a legislative body based on suffrage and attended by the highest guarantees of independence and purity. [85]

Had the dictator kept this promise, the new "elected legislative organ" might have made possible a satisfactory quasi-constitutional transition back to parliamentary government. This he did not do. On July 26, 1929, Primo declared that, in the course of time, the Draft Constitution would be submitted to the Spanish people by means of a plebiscite, which, he assured the King, was "the most sincere and the most democratic" procedure. [86] In other words, the Draft Constitution and other implementing legislation would, after being approved—and perhaps modified—by Primo, be offered to the Spanish people by plebiscite on a take-it-or-leave-it, yes-or-no basis, and then be submitted to the King for his aproval. Primo had decided that he would have nothing to do with a Cortes, which was sure to discuss, raise questions, and even amend the carefully contrived new constitution. Even in those days before Adolph Hitler, it was beginning to be evident that the plebiscite is a means whereby an "élite" makes a dishonest, over-simplified bid for the approval and support of the confused masses.

XI. Résumé: Political Concepts, Methods and Techniques, Achievements and Results

P RIMO de Rivera can hardly be said to have had a political program. He himself considered his rule patriotically apolitical. This *miles gloriosus* come to power sought in conceit and in prejudice compensation for his admitted ignorance of civil administration and for his willful naiveté in matters political. In lieu of adequate preparation, the dictator possessed an assortment of military habits, class prejudices, and a few liberal notions.

As a general and member of an Army family, the only social group organization of which Primo could conceive was a military type of hierarchy—disciplined, "apolitical," and inclined to action rather than to reflection and discussion. As a corollary, he was convinced that all politics and all politicians were harmful and vicious. Patriots need no political parties because they are inevitably all of one mind, and Primo was Spain's ranking patriot. Therefore, an opposition was not merely unnecessary; it was intolerable.

As for civilian organizations, Primo seemed to respect most the disciplined purposefulness of the socialist labor unions of the UGT. The régime's labor code encouraged further organization as well as additional economic gains at the expense of bourgeois entrepreneurs—who did not belong to the oligarchy anyway! Organized labor was favored so long as it did not lessen production.

77

On the other hand, anarchists and syndicalists, who sought to organize agricultural labor, constituted a threat to the political and economic position of the landowners and, therefore, were not to be tolerated. The régime's slightly progressive labor legislation was never made applicable to rural labor. But the interests of large-scale producers of grain and olive oil were protected by tariffs and import quotas.

On two important issues, Catalonian separatism and the Moroccan war, the dictator changed his mind completely, shortly after coming to power. At first he had favored autonomy for Catalonia as well as withdrawal from Morocco, but soon both patriotism and political pressures caused him to refuse to hear of Catalonian autonomy and to prosecute energetically the war in Morocco.

Among the liberal attitudes which Primo had acquired were: the slightly condescending feminism of a pseudo-liberal military Don Juan, a guilty respect for the suspended Constitution of 1876, and a conviction that his consultative National Assembly must be unicameral.

As regards administrative method, the régime manifested two distinct phases. First, the period of the Military Directory, September 15, 1923, to December 3, 1925, was held to be a temporary military occupation of Spain by the Spanish Army and Navy. Military and naval officers discharged the duties of civil functionaries.

During the second phase, which includes the year 1926 and on through 1929, the dictator ruled with the aid of a Ministerial Dictatorship. In setting up this consultative and administrative "cabinet," Primo replaced most of the generals with civilians. During these last four years, Don Miguel tried to utilize the Unión Patriótica for two purposes: first, to enlist mass support for his apolitical rule and, second, for the re-

78

cruitment of abler administrative personnel. It was impossible to attain fully either end because the organization was boycotted by so many Spaniards of prestige and integrity.

Chief among Primo's political techniques were the following:

Military coup and Putsch-in-reverse. With the approval or acquiescence of a great majority of the Spanish people, Don Miguel and his military associates assumed power in September 1923. The Putsch-in-reverse occurred in January 1930, when the dictator appealed in vain to the highest ranking generals for an informal vote of confidence in his régime.

The discrediting of all political parties and the ostracism of political leaders. The military's patriotic and apolitical government was to put an end to the iniquities of politics and politicians. However, in the latter years of his rule, Primo came to realize that he needed some of these very politicos and their followers to make acceptable his régime and party. But by that time such men either were in exile, were disaffected, or were working actively in the conspiratorial opposition.

Arbitrary control and coercion. The régime endeavored to exercise arbitrary and unlimited control over army officer promotion lists, over universities, professors, students, and cultural organizations, and over the judiciary. Arbitrary and entirely extra-legal fines were also imposed upon recalcitrant and politically unreliable citizens.

Censorship and the police power. Prior censorship of the press, vigilant policing, exile, and imprisonment were employed as "the shortest way with dissenters."

"Union" of all arms and services. His own creation, through mutiny, of an apolitico-military régime made Primo very sensitive to anything that might undermine military discipline. Ironically, it was the dictator's attempt to apply uniformity of discipline to the artillery officers which did most to create active opposition among the military.

79

Monopoly of patriotism. Primo's Unión Patriótica sought the support of all Spaniards of good will. At first, such patriots were expected to be monarchists; later, as tension between dictator and monarch increased, this requirement was ignored.

Party conventions and plebiscites. Party assemblies were convened to "hear and approve" the policies and decisions announced by the dictator and his advisers. In addition, the party sponsored and conducted carefully rigged pseudo-plebiscites designed to give the régime the appearance of having the almost unanimous approval of the Spanish people. More important than their dubious value as morale builders, such coerced *Ja*-votes humiliated and demoralized the opposition.

National Assembly. The consultative National Assembly, of membership largely appointive but in part elective, engaged in limited discussion, but could not effectively refuse approval of measures submitted to it by Primo or his advisers.

Draft of a new constitution. The *Anteproyecto de Constitución de 1929* was still under discussion when Primo fell from power. Its purpose was not only to eliminate from Spanish political life the ills peculiar to nineteenth century liberalism and parliamentarism but also to give to the régime status in terms of legality.

As regards achievement in a positive sense, the dictatorship was thought to have brought about the reestablishment of order, if not of law. Furthermore, cooperation with the French brought the Moroccan war to a relatively satisfactory conclusion. Also, the régime favored the organization and enhanced the prestige of urban labor.

However, the dictatorship also produced other results which can only be considered politically disastrous. It destroyed, for the time being at least, the pattern of representative, responsible government. In the main, the dictatorship fostered caste cleavage and class particularism and made more difficult,

80

almost impossible, the coexistence of the disparate elements of Spanish society. The monarchy was seriously undermined by its collaboration with an unsuccessful dictatorship. Also, the king's acceptance of absolutism made all but impossible return to any form of constitutional monarchy.

Furthermore, the dictatorship demonstrated conclusively the ineptness and social bankruptcy of the Spanish military in dealing with matters economic and political. Its attempt to set up an organization of apolitical patriots deliberately dispensed with the services of those most experienced and versed in public affairs. Its intransigence and inflexibility made systematic political and social life impossible, with the result that opposition was led to express itself by plotting and conspiring. Amply demonstrated also were the inadequacy of personal rule, the inefficacy of one-party political monopoly, and the indispensability of discussion and debate.

XII. In Conclusion: Collapse for Want of
an Opposition

I N Spain during the years 1923-30, General Primo de
  Rivera carried out his experiment in apolitical improvi-
zation under conditions more favorable than may ever occur
again. In the first place, parliamentary politics, as made
manifest in the Tweedledum-Tweedledee alternation in power of the "Conservative" and the "Liberal" pseudo-parties,
under the direction of their respective politicos, local machines,
and bosses, was in such ill-repute that the military dictatorship
was approved and welcomed by nearly all classes and groups,
except the dispossessed and ostracised political leaders. On the
other hand, the prestige of the military had not been so high
since the Peninsular War of 1808-1814. Unusual good luck
aided fumbling military genius to bring the Moroccan war to
a reasonably satisfactory conclusion. Primo was a national
savior who stayed on while his laurels faded.

General Primo de Rivera could only understand society in
terms of military organization. Furthermore, he did not understand politics and he, therefore, hated and distrusted all political parties and their leaders. From simple-minded militarism
and resentful anti-politicism stemmed his great defect as a national leader: that is, his complete inability to understand the
nature, significance, use, and importance of an opposition. The
term opposition, as here used, must include that of both types:
"His Majesty's loyal oppositon," as well as opposition of the
dirty, dishonest, underhanded, bushwhacking type. Each kind

has its uses, and the worse is better than none. For Primo, either kind of opposition was intolerable. His self-righteousness had given his dictatorship a monopoly, in his eyes, of virtue and good intentions. His superficial and impulsive approach to all problems caused him to assume that in each case there could be but one answer or solution, his solution, and no other. There could be no such thing as an honest difference of opinion. Refusal to agree with your superior—and Primo was the "superior" of all Spaniards, with the doubtful exception of King Alfonso XIII—was indiscipline, and indiscipline was akin to treason.

The Patriotic Union, Primo's self-righteous monopoly of apolitical patriotism, tended to set up a state within a state, and anyone who was not a member of this one party was not a Spanish citizen but a second-class subject with the choice of becoming a helot or an outlaw. Enforced acceptance of the régime's views and attitudes called for still wider use of police and security service, as well as censorship of all means of communication and of education.

Men, such as José Calvo-Sotelo and Gabriel Maura-Gamazo, who were practical politicians as well as political theorists well disposed toward Primo, have said that the dictator's great error was that he did not endeavor to convoke a true parliament. This is another way of saying that the régime failed for lack of an opposition. And this statement is neither a jest nor a paradox. For the functions of free, unhindered opposition are three:

First, freedom to express opposition is a safety valve whereby accumulated criticism, resentment and ill-humor are made harmless and often even useful;

Second, an organized opposition, articulate in press and parliament, is the anvil complementary to the hammer of the responsible party-in-power, for both anvil and hammer are essential to the forging of viable national policies;

84

Third, only through the joint labor of government and opposition can there come into being alternative measures and policies, ready for implementation and understood by the citizens, policies and measures which may take the place of some cabinet program which has proven to be unsatisfactory.

But General Primo de Rivera does not stand alone in having regarded an opposition as a political nuisance and liability, instead of as a social resource. Like so many others, before, since and now, he imagined that, by using force to impose arbitrary rule, he could abolish all opposition and so create the perfect state.

APPENDIX

Translations of Documents

1923: BARCELONA MANIFESTO

TO THE COUNTRY AND TO THE ARMY

SPANIARDS:

For us arrived the moment more feared than hoped for (because we should have desired that we might ever live within legality and that legality should without interruption rule over Spanish life); the time has come to give heed to the anxiety, to respond to the urgent demands of all those who, loving the mother country, see for her no other salvation than deliverance from the professional politicians, from the men who, for one reason or another, offer us the spectacle of the misfortunes and corruption which began in the year 1898 and which threaten Spain with an early end that will be both tragic and dishonorable. The thick net of politics of greed has caught in its meshes and has misdirected even the will of the Monarch. Frequently they seem to ask that the nation be governed by those who, they say, will not let others govern, thereby alluding to those who have been their only, albeit feeble, restraint and who brought to laws and customs the bit of healthy ethics and the slight tinge of morality and equity which they still have; but in reality they easily and contentedly agree to alternation in power and division of spoils, and together they themselves determine the order of succession in power.

Well then, we shall now assume entire responsibility and the nation shall be governed by us or by civilians who represent our morality and our principles. Enough, now, of gentle rebellions which, without remedying anything, damage as much or more than that strong and virile discipline to which we ardently devote ourselves for Spain and for the King.

This is a movement of men; let him who is not entirely sure of his complete masculinity await, quietly and in a corner, the good days which we are preparing for the Fatherland. Spaniards! Long live Spain and long live the King!

We do not have to justify our act, which the uncorrupted people demand and require. The murder of prelates, ex-governors, civil officials, employers, foremen, and workmen; bold and unpunished hold-ups; depreciation of currency, the squandering of millions from special funds, a customs policy suspect in its purpose, especially so since those who administer it flaunt their insolent immorality, base political intrigues having as their pretext the tragedy of Morocco, indecisiveness in confronting this most serious national problem, social indiscipline which makes work inefficacious and fruitless and which makes agri-cultural and industrial production uncertain and ruinous; unpunished communist propaganda, impiety and misbehavior, justice influenced by politics, shameless propaganda in favor of regional separatism, tendentious passions relative to the problem of responsibilities for the disaster in Morocco, and finally—l et us be just—one single count in favor of the government, which has survived for nine months thanks to the inexhaustible kindness of the Spanish people, a feeble and in-complete campaign against the vice of gambling.

We have not come to bewail shame and disgrace, but to apply a prompt and radical remedy, for which we demand the support of all good citizens. To this end, and by virtue of the confidence and man-date given me, there will be constituted in Madrid a military Director-ate of Supervision and Inspection, of a temporary character, charged with maintaining public order and insuring the working of the Min-istries and official bodies, requiring of the country that, in a short time, it offer us men upright, wise, industrious, and honorable who can constitute a Ministry under our auspices, but with complete independence of action, in order that we may offer them to the King if he sees fit to accept them.

We do not wish to be ministers nor have we any ambition other than that of serving Spain. We are the *Somatén,* the organized mi-litia of legendary and honorable Spanish tradition, and, like it, we have as our motto, "Peace, peace, and peace!"; but that means an honorable peace abroad and, at home, a peace based upon salutary sever-ity and just punishment. Let there be neither betrayal of principle nor impunity. We want a Somatén militia as a reserve and a brother to the Army in all things, including defense of the independence of the Fatherland if that should be threatened; but we want it even more in order to organize and line up men of good will so that their adhesion will strengthen us. In only a few days there will be issued the decree of organization of the Great Spanish Somatén.

We propose to avoid the shedding of blood and although, logically, no clean, pure, patriotic person will oppose us, we declare that faith in our ideals and the instinct of preservation of our régime will lead us to proceed with the greatest rigor against those who oppose it.

We wish to live at peace with all peoples and to merit from them, today, respect for the Spanish people; tomorrow, we expect to deserve from them admiration for our culture and virtues. We are not imperialists, nor do we hold that upon a stubborn insistence in Morocco depends the honor of the Army, for that honor is vindicated daily by valorous conduct. To this end, and when that Army shall have carried out the orders which it had received (for the Army was entirely unaware of this movement, which, although so lofty and noble, must not hinder the august mission of those who are facing the enemy at the front), then shall we seek for the Moroccan problem a solution that will be prompt, worthy, and reasonable.

The country does not want to hear more talk about responsibilities, but does want to know them and demand for them a prompt and just accounting, and this we shall entrust, subject to a time limit, to tribunals of moral authority which are impartial as regards everything which, up to now, has been poisoned by politics or ambition. The collective responsibility of the political parties we shall punish by this total interdiction from public life to which we condemn them, although in justice we recognize that some of their men devoted their talents to the noble activity of governing, but they never were able or did not want to purify and give dignity to the field of activity in which they have lived. We do want to do this because we think it our duty and, on receipt of any duly substantiated accusation of collusion, bribery, or immorality, we shall prosecute and punish implacably those who have offended against the mother country by corrupting and dishonoring her. We guarantee that accusations will be received in absolute confidence, although they be against persons of our profession and class, although they be against us ourselves, for there are accusations which do one honor. The prosecution of Don Santiago Alba begins at once, for he is accused by the unanimous voice of the country, and also to be prosecuted is he who was Premier [Manuel García-Prieto], who had heard from responsible persons in authority the most serious charges against his cynical and depraved Minister, and had even admitted the truth of these accusations, but

91

who, yielding to political influence and adroitness, did not have the character or integrity to prosecute him, or even to eliminate him from the Cabinet.

A manifesto does not admit of further details. Our work will very soon be known, and the nation and history will judge it, for our conscience is at rest as regards our purpose and intent.

DIRECTIVES:

When military law is declared in each military region, the Captain General or his substitute will expel from office all civil governors and will entrust their functions to the military governors and commandants. They will take possession of all telephone exchanges and means of communication and, except for personal and business messages, they will not permit communication by any official who does not serve the new régime.

All important happenings they will report in duplicate to the Captains General of Madrid and of Barcelona, and they will, on their own responsibility, cope promptly and energetically with any difficulties.

Appropriate places will be occupied, such as communist or revolutionary centers, railway stations, banks, electric power stations, and reservoirs, and persons suspect and of ill-repute will be placed under arrest. Otherwise, an impression of normal, tranquil life is to be created.

Until order is assured and the new régime triumphant, the military of all ranks and grades will give first attention to organization, vigilance, and public order, and all training or other act interfering with these objectives must be suspended, without this meaning that the troops are to be permitted to get soft or to abandon their professional mission.

Above all other instructions are the measures which will be suggested by patriotism, intelligence, and enthusiasm for the cause, in moments when one must not hesitate but risk all for all, that is to say, risk his life for the Fatherland.

Just a few words more. We have not conspired. We have, in broad daylight, championed the aspirations of the people and we have given them something in the way of organization, in order to direct them toward a patriotic end devoid of ambitions. We believe, then, that no one will act insolently toward us and, therefore, we have omitted asking, one by one, for the support of our colleagues and subordinates. In this holy undertaking are associated, in the first place, industrious and upright people of all classes, the Army and our glorious Navy, both of these down to their lowest ranks, which we could not have consulted previously without relaxing the bond of discipline, but who assure us of their valued and efficacious support because of their well-known loyalty to their officers and their sensitivity to patriotic aspirations.

Although we may come into being through an act of technical indiscipline, we do represent that true discipline which is due our principles and love of country, and so we shall conceive, practice, and require discipline, not forgetting that, since we are not moved by ambition but, on the contrary, by the spirit of sacrifice, ours is the highest authority.

And now, again, Long live Spain and long live the King! and receive, all of you, the cordial greeting of an old soldier who asks of you discipline and fraternal union, in the name of the days he shared military life with you in peace and in war, and who asks of the Spanish people trust and order, in the name of his efforts devoted to its prosperity, especially in the name of this undertaking in which he offers and risks all in order to serve the people.—MIGUEL PRIMO DE RIVERA, Captain General of the 4th Region. Barcelona, September 12, 1923.

1928: PLATFORM OF THE PATRIOTIC UNION

FATHERLAND, RELIGION, MONARCHY

But if the significance of these three words should be considered excessively ample or diffuse, and if we should be accused of lack of concreteness with regard to doctrine, aspirations, and commitments, I am going to specify, in numerical order for greater definiteness, the chief points to which our League devotes special attention, ascribing to them an independent existence:

1st. The promulgation of a new constitutional law and of the appropriate complementary laws which, in addition to serving as a guarantee of the principles enunciated in the motto, will assert the concept of national unity, sovereignty of the State, and the organization of a parliamentary régime based upon a single chamber legislature, in which shall have voice, vote, and joint representation People, Crown, State, and government sponsored guilds, with abolition of any electoral systems by districts, which is the base and proven source of demoralizing boss rule.

2nd. That for the approval of the new fundamental Code of the State, the plebiscite be employed as a representation of the direct vote of the citizenry, all bond, similarity, and connection with the opprobrious past, its forms and procedures being rejected.

3rd. To maintain at all cost, as fixed and permanent basis of the national economy, the balanced budget and the commitments of amortization of public debts as provided by law.

4th. To set up a system of renting and acquisition of rural property, which, without injury or damage to the primary rights of the land-owners, will permit the gradual grant to individuals or groups of dem-

95

onstrated capacity for it the ownership or maintenance of the lease in form such that it will assure to them just participation in the improvements due to their efforts. All delay in setting up and perfecting, serenely and methodically, such system, in addition to being a flagrant injustice, will contribute to the incubation of germs of revolution in the countryside, which can only be avoided, to the benefit of all, by a forward-looking agrarian law, applied by a government of highest authority.

5th. To foster through thrift and cooperatives, together with the aid and sponsorship which the State should lend to work of such indisputable importance, the increase in the amount of cheap and moderately-priced housing and the acquisition of farms, since this, aside from furthering the periodic and indispensable renovation of the great cities and intensifying country life, will keep forming, in the quiet of the the home and amid the security of property and shelter, feelings of brotherhood and social relationship, which will stimulate the defense of collective interests as a safeguard of those of the individual.

6th. To organize, with the required cooperation of the worker, the employer, and the State, insurance against unemployment, old age, and being incapacitated, so that no citizen who has expended his strength in labor may ever be found in the sad and embarrassing situation of having to beg his daily bread.

7th. To encourage and favor vertical guild organization to the end that all activities may be grouped in accordance with that system, not only for the purpose of appropriate, defined and clear representation at specified times, but as a means of settling harmoniously the differences and disagreements which arise in social life.

8th. Elementary schooling with complete religious and patriotic instruction, obligatory and organized on such a scope that it may be received without exception by all minors of both sexes before the age of eleven years; such instruction to be entrusted, without undue influence of special doctrines or organizations, to the personnel most adequate for its diffusion, according to the capacity of each, undertaking to put an end to illiteracy with such energy and example that each Spaniard will consider as the highest and most meritorious achievement the fact of having himself taught a fellow citizen to read and write.

9th. Military organization which will permit, within the shortest possible period of instruction, adequate individual training of recruits and the creation of district schools for specialist, cadre, and command practice, so that the system remains associated with that of national physical education and premilitary training, needs for matériel for a general mobilization having been met, however.

10th. Prosecution of the work of making our Naval personnel efficent because of the types and condition of their matériel and because of a high standard of instruction.

11th. Vigilant attention and spiritual, civic, and economic aid to the organizations of colonies of Spaniards abroad.

12th. Ever closer spiritual, intellectual, and mercantile relations with the countries of Iberian origin, so that, while the nations preserve the characteristics of their independence, they consider themselves included, especially during difficult moments in world affairs, in a great League which is to be a sort of comprehensive expression of the genius and the duties of the [Hispanic] race and is to tend primarily to the maintenance of peace and justice.

13th. Intervention in national production and in the sale of its products, in order to avoid usury or ruinous domestic competition, undertaking to guarantee the quality of the articles and products exported, in order that the reputation of Spanish business for integrity may not decline and that the national prestige may not suffer.

14th. A system of commercial treaties adjusted to the necessities and circumstances of this country and to the required and appropriate reciprocity with the contracting nations.

15th. Tenacious and diligent conduct of public works undertaken and approved, until there can be received from them the use and benefits which inspired their undertaking.

16th. Strengthening the system of administrative decentralization and autonomy of the provinces and townships (municipios), following closely the course indicated in the Statutes which govern them, and which, with the grants of taxes which are entrusted to them, will make of these organisms (which are so closely in touch with all social classes and so familiar with the surrounding interests which make up the general interest) powerful promoters of the enrichment of Spain by firmly uniting them morally and materially with the life of the State.

17th. Inflexibility in exacting the fulfillment of their duties by all public functionaries, providing them with means for an independent and worthy life, but reducing their number by organic simplification and by increase of work load up to the legal maximum.

18th. Persistent propaganda, everywhere and at all times, until a change in habits is achieved, inspired in the most healthful ethical principles and in the precepts of hygiene, which, without depriving our country of its unique aspect of joy and optimism, will convert it into an insuperable example of industry and orderly life.

19th. To surround woman with ever greater manifestations of respect, by granting her the participation which she deserves in social life; to give more tender care to children and more positive and efficacious protection to the humble, not only by means of institutions devoted to such high objectives, but also by taking advantage of all circumstances to preserve in the people their fine sensibility.

And the last point to be stated concretely, which should have been the first: To proceed tenaciously and inflexibly with the cleansing of the august functions entrusted to Justice at all its levels, undertaking the radical reform of the laws of Procedures, and giving to the citizens, more than the sensation, the absolute guarantee that justice in Spain has come to be upright, prompt, understanding, cheap, and invulnerable to all influences.[87]

1930: VOTE OF CONFIDENCE REQUESTED

Since the dictatorship came into being through proclamation by the military, interpreting, in my opinion, sound aspirations of the people, who did not delay in showing their enthusiastic adhesion which, now increased, the dictatorship believes it still retains, the dictatorship (inasmuch as the people's attitude is not easy to establish rapidly and with numerical exactness, as is that of the military) submits itself to the opinion of the military, and authorizes and urges the ten Captains General, the Supreme Chief of the forces of Morocco, three Captains General of maritime departments, and Directors of the Civil Guard, Customs Guards, and Disabled Veterans, that after a brief, discreet, and confidential consultation and investigation, which should not descend below the level of chiefs of units and services, they transmit their conclusion in writing and, if they prefer, that they meet in Madrid in order to reach a decision under the chairmanship of the ranking member of the group, and that they state whether the dictatorship continues to deserve the confidence and good opinion of the Army and the Navy. If the dictatorship does not enjoy their confidence, within five minutes after learning that fact, the powers of the Chief of the dictatorship and the government will be returned to His Majesty the King, because from him he received them on becoming the interpreter of the will of the military.

And now I only ask of my companions in arms and rank that they consider this note as a personal communication sent directly to them and that, without loss of a minute, they decide and communicate their attitude, for they will certainly understand how delicate is the situation which this step (the gravity of which I am not unaware of) creates for the régime over which I preside. First and foremost, it was the Army and the Navy which set me up as dictator, some with their adhesion, others with their tacit consent. The Army and the Navy are the first summoned to declare sincerely whether I should continue being dictator or whether I ought to resign my powers.[88]

99

NOTES

●

I. MILITARY CAREER OF MIGUEL PRIMO DE RIVERA

1. According to some reports, Don Miguel was the protagonist of another exploit which definitely was not entered on his service record. "The only officer casualty in a small Moroccan campaign in 1893 was the Commander-in-Chief, General Margallo. Actually he was shot with a revolver by a young lieutenant, Miguel Primo de Rivera, later the dictator, who was indignant that the rifles with which the Moors were killing Spanish soldiers had been sold to them surreptitiously by the General." (Gerald Brenan, *The Spanish Labyrinth*, p. 61, note 2. Mr. Brenan gives as his source Manuel Ciges Aparicio, *España bajo la dinastía de los Borbones*, Madrid, 1932.)

II. PERSONALITY AND ATTITUDES OF THE DICTATOR

2. G. Brenan, *The Spanish Labyrinth*, pp. 78-79.
3. Jérome et Jean Tharaud, *Rendez-vous espagnols*, Paris, 1925, p. 48.
4. José Ortega y Gasset, *España invertebrada* (1921), in his *Obras completas*, v. 3, Madrid, 1947, pp. 51-85. English translation: *Invertebrate Spain*, New York, 1937, pp. 19-57; the English version differs somewhat from the Spanish.
5. M. Primo de Rivera, *El pensamiento de Primo de Rivera*, Madrid, 1929, p. 354. From the first of three articles which Primo wrote for the United Press in February 1929. Henceforth, this collection of speeches, proclamations, press releases, etc., which was edited by José María Pemán, will be referred to as *"Pensamiento."*
6. For example, Eduardo Aunós, Minister of Labor under Primo and, later, of Grace and Justice under General Franco: "In his make-up as a XIXth century liberal, parliamentary structuration is considered unalterable..." (E. Aunós, *Primo de Rivera, soldado y gobernante*, Madrid, 1944, p. 158.)
   Also, in a lecture in Madrid, March 15, 1947: "The ideology of General Primo de Rivera as chief obstacle to his work. General Primo de Rivera was restrained by one prime political consideration.. To no one is it a mystery that the Marquis of Estella was fundamentally a liberal. He passed his life amid principles, theories, and facts of liberal significance." (Reprinted in E. Aunós, *Semblanza política del general Primo de Rivera*, Madrid, n. d., pp. 28-29.)

101

III. LAND, LABOR, CAPITAL — AND THE MILITARY

7. See Antonio Ramos-Oliveira, *Historia de España*, Mexico City, 1950, v. 2, pp. 338-341 and 432-478.
8. Himself a member of a landowning family, Don Miguel was prejudiced against all anarchists. He did, however, agree that the lot of the Andalusian agricultural day-laborers was hard, but asserted that their efficiency was too low to justify any increase in pay. (From an article of August 20, 1924, in answer to Largo-Caballero's criticism of the social irresponsibility of the *señoritos*, the Andalusian landowners. See *Pensamiento*, pp. 124-127.)
9. These were: *Consejo Interventor de Cuentas del Estado* (Council of Audit and Control of State Accounts), *Comisión Interina de Corporaciones* (Interim Commission on Corporate Bodies), *Consejo del Trabajo* (Labor Council), and *Consejo de Estado* (Council of State). See A. Ramos-Oliveira, *Historia*, v. 2, p. 473.

IV. THE BARCELONA MANIFESTO OF SEPTEMBER 1923

10. *Pensamiento*, pp. 20-22.
11. For an English translation of the entire Manifesto, see Appendix, pp. 89-93.
    The Spanish text will be found in *Pensamiento*, pp. 19-24; also, in Enrique Díaz-Retg, *España bajo el nuevo régimen*, pp. 85-92, and in Francisco Hernández-Mir, *La dictadura ante la historia*, Madrid, 1930, pp. 64-70.

V. MILITARY DIRECTORY AND MINISTERIAL DICTATORSHIP

12. E. Díaz-Retg, *España bajo el nuevo régimen*, p. 98.
13. A. Ramos-Oliveira, *Historia*, v. 2, p. 482.
14. The Count of Romanones was fined half a million pesetas, nearly a hundred thousand dollars; General Francisco Aguilera, 200,000 pesetas; General Valeriano Weyler and Dr. Gregorio Marañón, 100,000 pesetas each; the anarchist lawyer, Eduardo Barriobero, 15,000; the republican leader, Marcelino Domingo, 5,000; two newspaper men, 2,500; and an anarcho-syndicalist leader, 1,000 pesetas. See Gabriel Maura-Gamazo, *Al servicio de la historia*, v. 1, p. 321.
15. Involved in this conspiracy of 1929 were liberals, who desired a constituent Cortes to reestablish constitutional government, and generals, who merely sought an end to a dictatorship which, they held, was misgoverning Spain in the name of the Army. For details, see Antonio Ballesteros, *Historia de España*, Barcelona, 1936, v. 8, p. 630, and, especially, F. Hernández-Mir, *La dictadura*, Madrid, 1930, pp. 343-360.
16. For a translation of this circular, see Appendix, p. 99.

VI. AN ERA OF GOOD FEELING

17. For Costa, in the year 1901, *Jesús, cirujano de hierro*, who drove the money changers from the temple, was the prototype of the violent and severely just dictator who would bring social and political reforms to a demoralized Spain. See J. Costa, *Crisis política de España*, 3d ed., Madrid, 1914, p. 75.

18. A. Ramos-Oliveira, *Historia,* v. 2, p. 459.
19. Eduardo Aunós, *España en crisis (1874-1936),* Buenos Aires, 1942, pp. 272-273.
20. A. Ballesteros, *Historia,* v. 8, p. 607.
21. A. Ramos-Oliveira, *Historia,* v. 2, p. 457. This was the official position of the Socialists as a political party. However, such socialist labor leaders as Francisco Largo-Caballero and Manuel Llaneza of the UGT worked out a *modus operandi* with Primo. "There is nothing to fear," said Llaneza, Asturian chief of the coal miners' union, after his first interview with the dictator in 1923.

VII. PROBLEMS AND DIFFICULTIES

22. *Pensamiento,* p. 195. From an address to the Uniones Patrióticas at the Palacio de Hielo, Madrid, October 16, 1925.
23. May 26, 1924. *Ibid.,* p. 214.
24. From a speech in the Teatro del Centro, Madrid, March 8, 1924. *Ibid.,* p. 259.
25. José Pemartín, *Los valores históricos en la dictadura española,* Madrid, 1928, pp. 597-601.
26. Gabriel Maura-Gamazo, *Al servicio,* v. 1, p. 269.
27. *Ibid.,* v. 2, p. 67. The monarchist politician, Gabriel Maura-Gamazo, eldest son of the XIXth century political leader, Don Antonio Maura, is Duke of Maura as well as Count of Mortera. Gabriel is not to be confused with his brother Miguel, who was a republican.
28. Cited by F. Hernández-Mir in *La dictadura ante la historia,* p. 116.
29. G. Maura-Gamazo, *Al servicio,* v. 1, pp. 43-44.
30. From an address before an officers' banquet, February 25, 1924; reprinted in *Pensamiento,* p. 237.
31. See the address to the Círculo de la Unión Mercantil de Madrid of February 16, 1925, and the "Ice Palace speech" of October 16 of that year, as reproduced in part in *Pensamiento,* pp. 253 and 189.
32. G. Maura-Gamazo, *Al servicio,* v. 1, pp. 194-197.
33. F. Hernández-Mir, *La dictadura,* p. 193.
34. A. Ballesteros, *Historia,* v. 8, p. 629.
35. F. Hernández-Mir, *La dictadura,* p. 341.
36. *Diccionario de historia de España,* Madrid, 1952, v. 2, p. 917.
37. *Pensamiento,* p. 65. From an article in *La Nación,* Madrid, August 6, 1927.
38. *Ibid.,* p. 203. From an address at a banquet of homage to the King, Madrid, January 22, 1925.
39. *Ibid.,* pp. 23-24. Also, E. Díaz-Retg, *España bajo el nuevo régimen,* pp 91-92.
40. *Ibid.,* p. 227.
41. *Ibid.,* p. 233. From an address before the Army and Navy Officers' Club of Barcelona, February 1, 1925.
42. *Ibid.,* pp. 109 and 53. The Spanish texts are as follows:
"... *en el partido caben cuantos acaten la Constitución del 76*" (p. 109), and "*Deben integrarla* (la Unión Patriótica), *todos los que acepten la Constitución de 1876. —Es decir, cuantos acepten y acaten los preceptos contenidos en el Código fundamental de la nación*" (p. 53). The dictator's

use of the discreet word *acaten*, from *acatar*, "to revere" or "to accept with due respect, homage, and submissive reverence," is reminiscent of the way in which the XVIIth century colonial bureaucracy circumvented the enlightened provisions of the Laws of the Indies; the consecrated phrase was: *La ley se acata, pero no se cumple*, "The law is revered but it is not observed." Even so General Primo de Rivera in the XXth century.

43. *Ibid.*, p. 36. Manifesto of September 5, 1926.
44. *Ibid.*, p. 221.
45. Spaniards refer to this document as the *Anteproyecto de Constitución de 1929*. It was never adopted.
46. G. Maura-Gamazo, *Al servicio*, v. 2, p. 321; also, E. Aunós, *España en crisis*, p. 309.
47. From Alcides Arguedas, *Los caudillos bárbaros*, (The Barbarous Chieftains), as translated by Harriet de Onís, and included in Germán Arciniegas, *The Green Continent*, New York, 1944, p. 222.
48. Barcelona Manifesto of September 12, 1923.
49. E. Aunós, *Primo de Rivera*, p. 199.
50. *El Debate* of Madrid, October 6, 1929.
51. Salvador de Madariaga, *Spain*, London, 1942, p. 255.
52. *Justificación de la censura*, November, 1924; in *Pensamiento*, p. 169.
53. *Ibid.*
54. *Ibid.*, p. 171.
55. Air Force Major Ramón Franco, always a militant republican, was a member of the Constituent Cortes of the Spanish Republic in 1931.
56. A brief semi-official or "inspired" report of this incident omits all reference to the slight to the touchy General. It may be found in a book by Primo's admirer, José Pemartín, *Los valores históricos*, p. 85, note 9: "Principal penalties imposed upon the press ... *La Epoca* was fined 25,000 pesetas and suspended, for publishing a tendentious and evil-intentioned article about the homage accorded the aviators of the *Plus Ultra*. This fine was reduced by half, due to the intercession of the noted journalists, Don Torcuato Luca de Tena and Don Angel Herrera, and was paid directly into the funds of the social service organizations and the philanthropic religious orders."

VIII. APOLITICAL POLITICS

57. *Pensamiento*, pp. 207-208.
58. *Ibid.*, pp. 289 and 353.
59. *Ibid.*, p. 339.
60. See, especially, the following: *Ibid.*, "La Unión Patriótica," pp. 51-86 et passim; J. Pemartín, *Los valores históricos*, pp. 623-647; José María Pemán, *El hecho y la idea de la Unión Patriótica*, Madrid, 1929, pp. 5-116; and E. Díaz-Retg, *España bajo el nuevo régimen*, pp. 433-477.
61. *Pensamiento*, pp. 197 and 19.
62. *Ibid.*, p. 51.
63. *Ibid.*, p. 189.
64. From an address to the U. P. in Valladolid, on January 25, 1925. See *Ibid.*, p. 197, and G. Maura-Gamazo, *Al servicio*, v. 2, p. 145.
65. Primo in *La Nación* of August 6, 1927; in *Pensamiento*, p. 62.

66. Julián Cortés-Cavanillas, *La dictadura y el dictador,* Madrid, 1929. pp. 159-163.
67. *Pensamiento,* p. 63. From an article by Primo in *La Nación,* August 6, 1927.
68. *Ibid.,* p. 79.
69. *Ibid.,* pp. 58-61 and 78-82.
70. E. Aunós, *España en crisis,* pp. 300-310, and *Primo de Rivera,* pp. 177-180.
71. G. Maura-Gamazo, *Al servicio,* p. 247 et passim.

IX. TOWARD LEGALITY: THE NATIONAL ASSEMBLY

72. *Pensamiento,* pp. 41 and 78. Such words, which are a favorite eliché of Hispanic dictators, are re-echoed in General Franco's "I am responsible before God and History!"
73. "Be not troubled by the futile murmur of idle opinion; for to God alone shalt thou render account of thy acts." (Cited by J. Cortés-Cavanillas in *La dictadura y el dictador,* p. 321.)
74. G. Maura-Gamazo, *Al servicio,* v. 1, p. 272; also, E. Díaz-Retg, *España bajo el nuevo régimen,* pp. 435-436.
75. J. Pemartín, *Los valores históricos,* pp. 636-637. The figure given by Enrique Díaz-Retg, on page 438 of his *España bajo el nuevo régimen,* is only 6,935,862. But surely no one will give a second thought to half a million *Ja*-votes more or less in such a well-run plebiscite! A few years ago, Generalissimo Franco won a similar popularity contest, but he did make it possible for a few thousand audacious Spaniards to vote against him.
76. Words of the National Assembly's presiding officer, Professor José Yanguas-Messía, at the opening session. (See G. Maura-Gamazo, *Al servicio,* v. 2, pp. 99-100.)
77. Participation was, however, advocated by the right wing socialist leader, Professor Julián Besteiro, who maintained that the new National Assembly was no more corrupt and unrepresentative than the old Chamber of Deputies, in which the Socialists had been represented for thirty years. (See A. Ballesteros, *Historia,* v. 8, p. 623.) Of course, Besteiro was thinking in terms of possible immediate political advantage, while Prieto was, no doubt, thinking of his party's moral authority and revolutionary prestige in competition with anarchists, anarcho-syndicalists, communists, and other parties of the left, who would be only too eager to hurl charges and taunts of "collaborator with reaction," "counter-revolutionary," "social fascist," and the like.
78. See A. Ballesteros, *Historia,* v. 8, p. 623; also, G. Maura-Gamazo, *Al servicio,* v. 2, pp. 81-92.
79. A. Ballesteros, *Historia,* v. 8, p. 624.
80. G. Maura-Gamazo, *Al servicio,* v. 2, pp. 76-110; also, E. Díaz-Retg, *España bajo el nuevo régimen,* pp. 440-448.
81. A. Ballesteros, *Historia,* v. 8, pp. 624-629; and G. Maura-Gamazo, *Al servicio,* v. 2, pp. 278-291.
82. *World Almanac* 1931, p. 710.

X. THE STILL-BORN CONSTITUTION OF 1929

83. Eduardo Ortega-Gasset, brother of the better-known José, said that the amendments would lead to the most complete monarchic absolutism. For a brief exposition of the background, as well as an English translation of the 37 articles, see "The New Spanish Constitution," in *Current History*, v. 28, no. 4, July 1928, pp. 644-647, by Professor Malbone W. Graham, Jr., of UCLA.
84. Compare the effects of New Deal labor legislation in the United States.
85. G. Maura-Gamazo, *Al servicio*, v. 2, pp. 99-100.
86. *Ibid.*, p. 285. See also the first and second planks of the 1928 platform of the Patriotic Union, Appendix, p. 95.

XI. RESUME

XII. IN CONCLUSION

APPENDIX

87. *Pensamiento*, pp. 72-76; June 23, 1928.
88. For the Spanish text of this clumsily worded statement, see: G. Maura-Gamazo, *Al servicio*, v. 2, pp. 333-334; F. Hernández-Mir, *La dictadura*, pp. 358-359; or E. Aunós, *Primo de Rivera*, pp. 198-199.

BIBLIOGRAPHY

●

I. Books

A. Reports by Participants:

Alvarez del Vayo, Julio, *Freedom's Battle*, Alfred A. Knopf, New York, 1940, xix, 381, viii pp.

Alvarez del Vayo, Julio, *The Last Optimist*, Viking Press, New York, 1950, x, 406 pp.

Aunós, Eduardo, *España en crisis (1874-1936)*, Librería del Colegio, Buenos Aires, 1942, 445 pp.

Aunós, Eduardo, *La política social de la dictadura y Contestación del Marqués de Guad-el-Jelú*, Real Academia de Ciencias Morales y Políticas, Madrid, 1944, 143 pp.

Aunós, Eduardo, *Primo de Rivera, soldado y gobernante*, Ed. Alhambra, Madrid, 1944, 240 pp.

Aunós, Eduardo, *La reforma corporativa del estado*, Biblioteca de Ideas y Estudios Contemporáneos, M. Aguilar, Editor, Madrid, 1935, 271 pp.

Aunós, Eduardo, *Semblanza política del general Primo de Rivera*, Gráficas Minerva, Madrid, 1947, 71 pp.

Aunós, Calvo Sotelo, et al., *Curso de ciudadanía*. Conferencias pronunciadas en el Alcázar de Toledo, Marzo 1929. Prólogo del general Primo de Rivera, Junta de Propaganda y Ciudadanía, Madrid, 1929, xi, 355 pp.

Berenguer, Dámaso, *De la dictadura a la república*, Ed. Plus Ultra, Madrid, 1946, 417 pp. (Preface dated October 1935).

Blasco Ibáñez, Vicente, *Alfonso XIII Unmasked*. Authorized translation by Leo Ongley, E. P. Dutton & Co., New York, 1924, 121 pp.

Calvo Sotelo, José, *Mis servicios al estado*. Seis años de gestión. Apunte para la historia, 1st ed., Imprenta Clásica Española, Madrid, 1933, 515 pp.

Díaz-Retg, Enrique, *España bajo el nuevo régimen*. Cinco años de gobierno de Primo de Rivera, 1923 - Septiembre - 1928, Ediciones Mercurio, Madrid, 1928, 480 pp.

Hernández-Mir, Francisco, *Un crimen de lesa patria, La dictadura ante la historia*. Prólogo de Joaquín Aznar, CIAP, Madrid, 1930, 361 pp.

107

López de Ochoa, Eduardo, *De la dictadura a la república,* Prólogo de Eduardo Ortega y Gasset, Ed. Zeus, Madrid, 1930, 265 pp.

Maura-Gamazo, Gabriel, *Al servicio de la historia.* Bosquejo histórico de la dictadura, 4th ed., 2 vols. Javier Morata, Madrid, 1930, 377 and 344 pp.

Maura-Gamazo, Gabriel, *Recuerdos de mi vida,* M. Aguilar, Madrid, 1934, 259 pp.

Maurín, Joaquín, *Los hombres de la dictadura:* Sánchez-Guerra, Iglesias, Largo Caballero, Lerroux, Melquiádes Alvarez, "Cenit," Madrid, 1930, 244 pp.

Ortega y Gasset, José, "España invertebrada", in *Obras completas,* Ed. Revista de Occidente, Madrid, 1947, vol. 8, pp. 37-128.

Ortega y Gasset, José, *Invertebrate Spain,* Norton, N.Y., 1937.

Ossorio, Angel, *Diccionario político español histórico y biográfico* (desde Carlos IV hasta 1936), Editorial Mundo Atlántico, Buenos Aires, 1945, 917 pp.

Pemán, José María, *El hecho y la idea de la Unión Patriótica.* Prólogo del general Primo de Rivera, Imprenta Artística, Sáez Hermanos, Madrid, 1929, 400 pp.

Pemartín, José, *Los valores históricos en la dictadura española.* Prólogo del general Primo de Rivera, Editorial Arte y Ciencia, Madrid, 1928, 658 pp.

Primo de Rivera, Miguel, *El pensamiento de Primo de Rivera.* Sus notas, artículos y discursos. Prólogo de José María Pemán, Imprenta Artística, Sáez Hermanos, Madrid, 1929, 374 pp.

Unamuno, Miguel de, *Romancero del destierro,* Editorial "Alba", Buenos Aires, 1928, 153 pp. (Poems).

B. *Other Reports From Direct Observation:*

Brenan, Gerald, *The Spanish Labyrinth,* An account of the social and political background of the civil war, Macmillan, New York, 1943, 384 pp.

"El Capitán Centellas" (pseudonym), *Las dictaduras y el señor Cambó,* Ed. Rubén Darío, Madrid, 1929, 184 pp.

Cortés Cavanillas, Julián, *La dictadura y el dictador,* Rasgos históricos, políticos y psicológicos, Talleres Tipográficos Velasco, Madrid, 1929, 356 pp.

Cuartero, José, *Artículos de don José Cuartero.* Homenaje de "ABC" a su insigne redactor. Prólogo de Torcuato Luca de Tena, Prensa Española, Madrid, 1947, 398 pp.

Finat Rojas, Hipólito, (Marqués de Carvajal), *Reflexiones del hombre de la calle.* ¿Cuál es el horizonte político de España?, Francisco Beltrán, Madrid, 1929, 308 pp.

Hoyos y Vinent, Antonio de, (Marqués de Vinent), *El primer estado.* Actuación de la aristocracia..., CIAP, Madrid, 1931, 252 pp.

Mora, Constancia de la, *In Place of Splendor.* The autobiography of a Spanish woman, Harcourt, Brace & Co., New York, 1939, 433 pp.

Primo de Rivera, José Antonio, *Obras completas de* ... Edición cronológica. Prólogo del Excmo. Sr. Ministro de Información, Don Gabriel Arias-Salgado, Publicaciones Españolas, Madrid, 1952, 1155 pp.

Tharaud, Jérome et Jean, *Rendez-vous espagnols,* Librairie Plon, París, 1925, 85 pp.

C. *Works on the Social and Political Background*:

Alcalá-Galiano, Alvaro, *La caída de un trono,* CIAP, Madrid, 1933, 269 pp.

Altamira, Rafael, *Historia de España,* 8 vols., Barcelona, 1919-1936.

Ansaldo, Juan Antonio, *¿Para qué?* De Alfonso XIII a Juan III, Editorial Vasca Ekin, S.R.L., Buenos Aires, 563 pp.

Arciniegas, Germán, *The Green Continent,* Knopf, New York, 1954, 535 pp.

Areilza, José María and Castiella, Fernando María, *Reivindicaciones de España.* Prólogo de Alfonso García Valdecasas, Instituto de Estudios Políticos, Madrid, 1941, 669 pp.

Ballesteros y Beretta, Antonio, *Historia de España y su influencia en la historia universal,* 8 vols., Salvat Editores, S.A., Barcelona, 1919-1936; vol. 8, pp. 603-631.

Brandt, Joseph A., *Toward the New Spain,* University of Chicago Press, Chicago, 1933, 435 pp.

Comín Colomar, Eduardo, *Un siglo de atentados políticos en España,* Madrid, 1951, 303 pp.

Costa, Joaquín, *Oligarquía y caciquismo como la forma actual de gobierno en España,* Madrid, 1902.

Diccionario de historia de España. Desde sus orígenes hasta el fin del reinado de Alfonso XIII, 2 vols., "Revista de Occidente", Madrid, 1952, 1566 & 1386 pp.

Foltz, Charles, *The Masquerade in Spain,* Houghton Mifflin, Boston, 1948, 375 pp.

García Escudero, José María, *De Cánovas a la República,* Ed. Rialp, S.A., Madrid, 1951, 356 pp.

Hamilton, Thomas J., *Appeasement's Child,* Knopf, New York, 1943, 327 pp.

Madariaga, Salvador de, *Spain,* Jonathan Cape, London, 1942, 509 pp.

Maura-Gamazo, Gabriel and Fernández Almagro, Melchior, *Por qué cayó Alfonso XIII,* Ediciones Ambos Mundos, Madrid, 1948, 545 pp.

Peers, E. Allison, *The Spanish Tragedy 1930-1936* Dictatorship, republic, chaos, Oxford University Press, New York, 1936, 247 pp.

Pérez Bustamente, C., *Síntesis de historia de España,* Ediciones Españolas, S.A., Madrid, 1939, 373 pp.

Ramos-Oliveira, Antonio, *Historia de España,* 3 vols., Cía. General de Ediciones, S. A., México City, 1950, 639, 652, and 640 pp.

Soncourt, Robert, *The Spanish Crown 1808-1931,* An intimate chronicle of a hundred years, Chas. Scribner's Sons. New York, 1932, 399 pp.

Verduin, Arnold R., *Manual of Spanish Constitutions 1808-1931,* Ypsilanti, Michigan, 1941, 99 pp.

II. PERIODICALS

Anonymous, "Siete años sin ley, España bajo la dictadura", 876 octavo pages; appeared serially in the Madrid daily, *El Sol,* from September 19, 1930 until March 24, 1933. (Installments appeared at irregular intervals after April 1931.)

(*Anteproyecto de Constitución de 1929.*) "Texto íntegro del Proyecto de Constitución", in *El Debate,* Madrid, vol. 19, No. 6233, Sunday, July 7, 1929, pp. 5-7. ("Síntesis", p. 1.)

Desmond, R. T., "The Aftermath of the Spanish Dictatorship", in *Foreign Affairs,* vol. 9, No. 2, Jan. 1931, pp. 297-309.

Graham, Jr., Malbone W., "The New Spanish Constitution", in *Current History,* N. Y. Times, vol. 8, No. 4, July 1928, pp. 644-647.

World Almanac and Book of Facts for 1931, *N. Y. World,* N.Y., 1931, 948 pp.

INDEX

111

112

113

TI DUE